COOPERATIVE EXTENSION

Establishing and Operating a Garden Center

REQUIREMENTS AND COSTS

EDITED BY

Susan S. Barton

WRITTEN BY

Susan S. Barton
Bridget Behe
Charles R. Hall
John J. Haydu
Roger A. Hinson
Robert E. McNiel
Travis D. Phillips
Russell D. Powell
Forrest E. Stegelin

Natural Resource, Agriculture, and Engineering Service (NRAES)
Cooperative Extension
PO Box 4557
Ithaca, New York 14852-4557

NRAES–161
December 2002 Revision

Inquiries invited. (607) 255-7654

ISBN 0-935817-86-7

Library of Congress Cataloging-in-Publication Data

Establishing and operating a garden center : requirements and costs / edited by Susan S. Barton ; written by Susan S. Barton ... [et al.].--2002 revision
p. cm. -- (NRAES ; 161)
Includes bibliographical references (p.).
ISBN 0-935817-86-7 (pbk.)
1. Garden centers (Retail trade) 2. Garden centers (Retail trade)--Cost of operation. I. Barton, Susan S. (Susan Schumacher), 1959- II. Natural Resource, Agriculture, and Engineering Service. III. NRAES (Series) ; 161.

SB454.6 .E78 2002
381'.4159'068--dc21

2002029586

Requests to reprint parts of this book should be sent to NRAES. In your request, please state which parts of the book you would like to reprint and describe how you intend to use the reprinted material. Contact NRAES if you have any questions.

Natural Resource, Agriculture, and Engineering Service (NRAES)
Cooperative Extension • PO Box 4557
Ithaca, New York 14852-4557
Phone: (607) 255-7654 • Fax: (607) 254-8770
E-mail: NRAES@CORNELL.EDU • Web site: WWW.NRAES.ORG

Contents

Part 2: Financial, Marketing, and Business Principles for Garden Center Operation

List of Tables

List of Figures

About the Authors

SUSAN S. BARTON *(Editor)*
Extension Specialist
Department of Plant and Soil Sciences
University of Delaware

Bridget Behe
Associate Professor
Department of Horticulture
Michigan State University

Charles R. Hall
Professor
Department of Agricultural Economics
The University of Tennessee

John J. Haydu
Professor
Mid-Florida Research and Education Center–Apopka
University of Florida

Roger A. Hinson
Professor
Department of Agricultural Economics and Agribusiness
Louisiana State University

Robert E. McNiel
Extension Professor
Department of Horticulture
University of Kentucky

Travis D. Phillips
Professor
Department of Agricultural Economics
Mississippi State University

Russell D. Powell
Area Extension Agent
The Pennsylvania State University

Forrest E. Stegelin
Associate Professor
Department of Agricultural and Applied Economics
University of Georgia

Preface

The S-290 Regional Research Project combines horticulturists with agricultural economists to look at issues important to the nursery industry.

Abstract

The objective of this book is to estimate establishment and operating costs for garden centers at two levels of sales and to specify the general set of financial, marketing, and business principles that should be available to the owner/manager of a garden center.

After surveying 25 garden centers across the United States, the authors derived two models for discussion: a large garden center with annual sales of $1,000,000 and a smaller garden center with annual sales of $350,000. Capital budgets, including investment and operations costs for each garden center, are developed. Each center is evaluated based on standard business indicators. A merchandising program composed of layout, pricing, advertising, cost structure, and diversification is outlined.

KEY WORDS: garden center, operating costs, product mixes, capital budgets, financial and income performance, merchandising program

Introduction

Since 1737, when William Prince established the first commercial nursery in the United States, there has been a need for a retail marketing channel in the nursery industry. As it has matured, the nursery industry has experienced considerable growth and marketing momentum.

In the 1990s, the nursery/greenhouse industry grew at an average annual rate of 4–5%. At $10.6 billion in 1998, it accounted for over 10% of all farm crop cash receipts. The nursery/greenhouse industry is made up of two major segments, floriculture and landscape horticulture, the larger being the nursery or landscape crops. Consumer expenditures for environmental horticultural products are approaching $38 billion annually (Johnson 1998).

Growth in the nursery industry has been in response to factors like rising real incomes, long-term increasing trends in housing starts, increasing costs of travel and other recreational options away from home, and tendencies of consumers to increase expenditures for home landscaping. In addition, growth has resulted from greater use of landscaping by industrial and commercial organizations, public and private institutions, and homeowners and residential renters. The population per establishment has decreased due to an increase in retail establishments. But the dramatic increase in per capita sales has allowed overall sales during the 1990s to continue to increase (table 1). While economic downturns experienced in the early 1990s and in 2001–2002 have slowed retail sales, opportunities exist for well-managed companies.

The increasing sales of ornamental plants has attracted the interest of several portions of the retail industry. The traditional garden center (offering plants, supplies, and hard goods) provided the outlet for these products for many years. However, the 1980s witnessed increased competition from other retail segments, particularly the mass merchandiser, as channels to the consumer. The rewholesaler and the landscape company also have become more important competitive segments. For these reasons, wholesale production nurseries and retail establishments have become more specialized, attempting to identify plants and production systems that provide a market niche that offers a competitive advantage.

Table 1. Selected data on retail nurseries and lawn-and-garden stores in the United States (selected years) [a/]

ITEM	1977	1987	1997
Number of firms	6,921	10,692	16,432
Sales (million) [b/]	$1,584	$5,412	$27,609
Average sales per firm	$228,939	$506,058	$1,680,180
Sales per employee	$43,578	$75,813	$198,428
Payroll per employee	$7,282	$11,518	$19,839
Payroll as percentage of sales	16.1	15.2	10.0 [c/]
Average number of employees [d/]	5.2	6.7	7.2
Population per establishment [e/]	31,822	22,815	16,294
Per capita sales [f/]	$7.19	$22.19	$103.12

Source: U.S. Bureau of Census, 1997 Economic Census

[a/] Establishments with payrolls
[b/] Sales excluded sales tax and finance charges.
[c/] Data from the 1998 Garden Centers of America operating cost study indicate a range of 18–22%.
[d/] Employees were full-time and part-time on the payroll for the week containing March 12.
[e/] Calculated by dividing resident population by number of firms
[f/] Calculated by dividing total sales by the resident population

RESEARCH PROBLEM

Firm size in the retail garden center industry is a continuum, including many small, locally owned and operated firms that capture a relatively small portion of sales and fewer large firms that capture the majority of sales. With the industry's growth, the number of actual and potential garden center entrepreneurs has increased. In at least some of these cases, the decision to invest in a garden center is based on a knowledge of and an interest in plants. Alone, this interest is insufficient to be successful—it must be combined with effective feasibility analyses and business management, financial planning, and marketing strategies.

There has been little research support to assist the entrepreneur in estimating the costs of establishing and operating a retail garden center. The literature is particularly bereft of economic information regarding the types of capital resources, costs, and procedures involved in developing, establishing, and operating such a business. The lack of information combined with impressive industry growth indicates a need to fill this void; hence, the impetus for this study.

OBJECTIVES

The overall objective of this analysis is to provide economic and technical information to potential and current garden center operators and managers, as well as members of the business community who work with garden centers, on the resources (financial and otherwise), costs, and procedures involved in establishing and operating a garden center. In this book, a garden center is defined as a retail outlet that handles green goods and hard goods. Green goods include all living plant materials and plant parts such as seeds, bulbs, and so forth. Hard goods are additional products related to the landscape and floral industries.

The specific research objectives were as follows:

1. Estimate establishment and operating costs for garden centers with two levels of sales by:
   A. Surveying existing garden centers to determine facility requirements, scale of operation, product mix, customer flows, marketing data, and related economic and financial information;
   B. Describing representative facilities, based on differences in business volume, physical layout, marketing strategy, and related factors; and
   C. Developing capital budgets, including investment and operations costs, for the representative firm sizes.
2. Specify the general set of financial, marketing, and business principles that should be available to and evaluated by the owner/manager of a garden center by:
   A. Evaluating the financial and income performance of the representative firms, compared to standard business indicators; and
   B. Developing a merchandising program composed of layout, pricing, advertising, cost structure, and diversification that contributes to business success.

DISCLAIMER

The numbers used for start-up costs and financial statements in this book are for illustration purposes only. They are not intended to reflect accurate estimates of the costs associated with establishing and operating a garden center. Garden center operators should use the charts and tables as guidelines for entering their own numbers to accurately reflect their own true costs. This book illustrates the methodology for using costs to calculate financial ratios and analyze business health.

PART 1: Establishment and Operating Costs of a Garden Center

MATERIALS AND METHODS

A survey of 25 garden centers was completed in 1990. These firms represented existing businesses whose primary activity was the retail sale of plants and complementary hard goods. The firms were of varying sizes, and they highlighted a cross-section of the United States in terms of climatological zones, population densities, plant species, disposable incomes, and market environments. Data collected included a description of the physical facilities, equipment and personnel requirements, product mix profiles, and marketing and financial evaluations.

Economic models were developed from the above information to describe one small and one large representative garden center. The representative small garden center's facilities and operations were sufficient to generate gross annual sales of $350,000. The larger retail garden center's facilities and operations were representative of a business having gross annual sales of $1 million. The large and small firms were modeled to portray realistic differences in the options available to garden center operators. Garden center managers can use this information as a menu to create unique models that resemble their own firms.

The economic analysis cites national average costs that individual operators may adjust to better reflect local or regional costs. The applicable capital investments in land, buildings and facilities, outdoor sales areas, and vehicles and equipment are described in later sections of this book. Operational expenses are also itemized for each of the two firms, emphasizing scalar costs like personnel, marketing margins, and product turnover.

Pro forma financial statements are developed for the model firms, and key financial measures are compared to those published in secondary business, financial, and economic sources. These financial and income performance evaluations ensure the reliability and accuracy of the model firms.

Industry-accepted marketing and managerial economic principles for achieving business success as a retail garden center are discussed. Emphasis is placed on the implementation and evaluation aspects of business management facilitating the profitability of well-managed, innovative, independent garden centers.

STARTING A BUSINESS

While prospective garden center investors may justify their proposals through a knowledge of and love for plants, that alone is not sufficient for achieving success. Before investing scarce resources, owners and/or managers must determine their potential as managers. Statistics consistently show that 80% of small businesses initiating retail activity will fail within the first five years of operation. Reasons for this failure rate often stem from a manager who does not have adequate experience, is unable to make decisions, is not self-starting or self-directed, is unorganized, is not a people person, and, in general, lacks business savvy and aptitude. Owning a small business can be demanding, and the owner must be prepared and willing to make the necessary commitment in terms of time, financial resources, and professional discipline.

Prior to committing money to a new business, or substantially altering the business's focus, the economic soundness of the proposal should be evaluated. Mistakes should be made "on paper" rather than at the expense of the business. Business assessment includes a market analysis and a feasibility study. In the market analysis, factors that directly influence the opportunity for success are analyzed, including competitor characteristics, demographics of the customer base, and market share potential. The feasibility analysis provides an evaluation of the specific site and includes an analysis of the business environment, such as availability of services, the store layout, cost estimates, turnover and sales estimates, and expected return on investment (ROI).

The bottom line on a feasibility study is whether or not the business venture will provide a higher ROI than alternative investments. Since starting a business involves more risk than most alternative investments, the difference in ROI should be large enough to compensate for the additional risk. If the feasibility study indicates that a garden center investment is sound, the process of structuring the business should continue.

By substituting their own numbers into the tables and appendixes in this book, garden center operators or potential operators can calculate the potential ROI. In the models chosen, new facilities with new equipment have been specified. For garden centers across the country, these numbers might change dramatically based on land costs, use of existing structures, purchase of used equipment, living costs, and other variables.

STRATEGIC PLANNING: DOES A POTENTIAL FOR SUCCESS EXIST?

A garden center exists in a competitive world with other garden centers and with mass merchandiser garden departments. Furthermore, consumers have any number of alternative ways to spend their money. Given this competition, the garden center operator should have an understanding of the basic forces that make firms and industries profitable (or unprofitable), of marketing, and of the many other factors that make a business successful. However, positioning and marketing are fundamental. Without the ability to attract customers and sell product, many other business skills become unimportant.

Basic competitive forces are important in determining the profitability of a firm or industry. These forces gauge the strength of the competitive situation in which the garden center will exist. When the forces are understood and analyzed, a business strategy can be chosen. The forces include the industry's structure (the number and size of firms) and the competition among firms. Different structures imply different strategies and subsequent marketing plans, including the sales target, price level, product mix, attributes of products, and provision of services. By analyzing structural characteristics of an industry and the strengths and weaknesses of individual firms, a competitive strategy can be developed to drive purchasing, operations, selling methods, and other major policies (Porter 1980).

The competitive forces that determine profitability of an industry and/or the nature of competition among firms in a market area are commonsense issues in a way, but their application is meaningful. If competition among firms within an industry is intense, profits will be bid away through price competition. If a garden center can shelter itself from such forces, it can be more profitable, holding other factors constant.

BASIC COMPETITIVE FORCES IN THE GARDEN CENTER MARKET

Entry/Exit of New or Different Firms into the Market

How easy is it for other firms to begin to offer competing products and services? If it is easy to get into the business and hard to get out, expect industry- and firm-level profits to be lower. Examples of entry barriers include high initial capital requirements or high associated risk. Garden centers face no institutional restrictions that prevent investment, but compliance with federal regulations and local/state ordinances and licensing is necessary.

Some factors related to entry are:

1. **Economies of scale.** Garden centers are capital-intensive. Larger garden centers generally have lower per-unit overhead or start-up costs based on using the same facilities, personnel, and equipment for more units. On the other hand, the industry contains many small and vibrant garden centers, suggesting that the cost advantages of large garden centers can be overcome through appropriate market strategy, location, and positioning.
2. **Switching costs.** These are the costs to the customer of leaving one business to patronize another. A customer might find that the combination of products and services being provided at one garden center is quite good. An alternative business would have to give customers sufficient reason to change their purchasing pattern. Some examples include accessibility, price, or service. Any developing garden center should study the products, services, and location of existing garden centers in terms of their ability to attract customers.
3. **Exit barriers can be important, too.** In a common example, getting out of an investment that is not performing as expected without loss of capital may not be possible. If the productive assets of the garden center have few alternative uses and could be sold only at a loss, there would be strong incentive to continue in business in the short run. Industry profitability may be reduced by such actions.

Substitutes

A garden center usually cannot expect to achieve high profits if there are good substitutes for the goods and services it provides. One of the few exceptions to this statement is the case of strong economic growth, where everyone is expanding. Still, if there is no other reason to choose one business over another, price will become the choice factor. Price competition drives down profits.

The successful garden center must distinguish itself from other garden centers and from mass merchandisers. Service and product knowledge are factors that might do the job. In addition to competing with other vendors of plant material and services, the garden center entrepreneur indirectly competes with a wide range of other goods and services.

Characteristics of some products make them more price-sensitive than others, and price-sensitive goods usually have a smaller markup. These are goods that (1) are standard, (2) comprise a significant portion of a customer's budget, and/or (3) are less important to the quality of the customer's gardening or landscaping project. These descriptions apply to many of the plants and products sold by garden centers, such as market packs of annuals, peat moss, one-gallon azaleas, and so forth. Though many price-sensitive products are stocked and used to attract customers, service level and product knowledge help to sell other items that are less price-sensitive (and carry a higher markup), such as flowering trees, statuary, and gift items. Specimen plants, although frequently not recognized nor appreciated as such, also command a price differential above the typical plant inventory.

Market Power of Buyers and Sellers

Buyers are the garden center's customers. Strong buyers (large purchasers, important customers, and so forth) have the power to influence prices and other terms of trade. Weak buyers are just the opposite.

The situation is much the same on the side of the sellers, or the garden center's suppliers. Sellers also affect the garden center's performance and profitability. The garden center's size relative to other firms determines how important it is, and important or strategic customers can bargain more effectively and achieve more control over cost and sales. Mass merchandisers that handle large volumes have more power than small garden centers. A customer is important to a seller when (1) it buys a significant portion of the supplier's output, (2) it is bigger than its suppliers, (3) the quantity purchased from a supplier is a large portion of cost, (4) the product is a standard one, or (5) the cost of changing suppliers is low.

For products that affect its image, the garden center would be less price-sensitive and have less room to negotiate. Small garden centers and garden centers just beginning in business may not have established credit and negotiating power with their suppliers. Established garden centers (large and small) can and do negotiate with some suppliers, primarily nurseries who supply them with plant material. However, their negotiation power is restricted when dealing with regional and national suppliers of hard goods.

Rivalry

Intense rivalries develop when gains by one firm mean losses for another. These situations may lead to intense price competition, which can depress profitability. Intense competition might occur when there is slow growth in a market; when firms have differing business objectives; when entry barriers are low; when exit barriers are high (high fixed costs, for example); or when cost of switching between suppliers is low. Or rivalry can occur based on personalities, when an owner of a marginal garden center might be stubborn and use low price as a way to attract customers. This could affect profitability of all sellers in that market area.

Rivalry among garden centers has been affected by three major trends. First, retail consolidation has occurred. Mass merchandisers continue to gain market share among many consumer groups, not just those whose objective is an inexpensive product. The traditional garden centers' share has declined. Second, individual garden centers, with their complement of facilities, are limited in their ability to capture economies of scale. This must be overcome in some way, such as the formation of buying cooperatives. And third, today's garden centers are more diversified, including more seasonal activities such as Christmas in their overall packages. These trends tend to increase competitive activity.

STRATEGIES THAT ADDRESS COMPETITIVE FORCES

Three general strategies that help a firm position itself are (1) cost leadership, (2) differentiation, and (3) focus.

Cost Leadership

Cost leadership is a primary defense against the four competitive forces. Low unit cost is achieved through size. The firm operates on a scale sufficient to capture available economies. New cost-reducing technologies are incorporated, and purchase costs are reduced by quantity discounts. Pricing is designed to retain and gain market share.

Differentiation

Unique characteristics can be the basis for being different from other retailers. The firm finds a way to stand out from the competition. High product quality is one approach. The differentiation may be broad, such as better overall service, a wider selection of plants, or a comprehensive guarantee policy. Or, a garden center might adopt a specific differentiation strategy. For example, a garden center located in a beach resort community might specialize in plants suitable for a beach landscape or instant landscaping for a second home.

Focus

This strategy involves choosing a particular portion of the market and finding ways to serve that segment well, while de-emphasizing other segments. A garden center focusing on a particular market segment would develop expertise and provide an improved set of services to that particular group of customers. The idea is to achieve superiority at some level or differentiation within its particular focus. Such segmentation would probably be more feasible in larger, upscale markets where incomes are sufficient to support specialized programs.

Selecting a Strategy

Each strategy provides offensive or defensive positioning against competitive forces in its own way. At the same time, each strategy has its drawbacks. For example, investment in technology required by the cost-leadership approach can place the firm in the position of high fixed costs with great expenses if it needs to switch to a new, more efficient methodology that unexpectedly develops. Focus can subject the firms to vagaries of the economy and market downturns in particular specialized segments. Finding the right place in the marketplace is a balance. None of the strategies can be implemented with total disregard for the others. As an example, a company that seeks to become a cost leader still must maintain a reputation for at least standard quality. But Porter (1980) warns that a company that does not choose a basic direction may find itself trying to pursue more than one strategy at the same time. In that case, customers cannot identify the company's core competencies, and the firm is "stuck in the middle," making tradeoffs among the strategies and doing none of them well.

Before selecting a strategy (cost leadership, differentiation, or focus), each garden center should analyze its own strengths and weaknesses and the market in which it will compete.

Mass merchandisers generally serve the low-priced end of the plant material market, using seasonal plant material as a complement to their usual lines of business. They price aggressively to attract attention. In addition to the mass merchandisers, some larger garden centers use a combination of specialization and volume through promotion of seasonal price-sensitive plants. In conjunction with multi-location operations, wide product lines, and advertising strategies that complement aggressive pricing, these large garden centers have lower average fixed costs through consolidated purchasing and transportation savings.

Given these factors, relatively small garden centers would be unlikely candidates for a cost-leadership strategy. However, either the differentiation or the focus strategy may provide excellent opportunities. Thorough analysis of market demographics will be necessary, but in the same way that specialty shops are located beside large department stores, there are economically viable niches that can be filled through good strategies.

The development of an image is a differentiation strategy, as it is based on public perception. A garden center in one location can operate with a high-quality, high-service image that accompanies its high price/margin structure. Another successful garden center in another location may choose to operate with a modest price/margin structure accompanied by a lower level of amenities but with other features that differentiate it from its competitors. Consistency of image presented to the community is important, since conflicting signals confuse customers.

The general strategies of focus and uniqueness have potential for smaller garden centers. Knowledge of the local market can be translated into advantage in the form of the green and hard goods product mix, service level, amenities offered, and pricing policy.

SUPPLY CHAIN MANAGEMENT AND OTHER STRATEGIES

Another consideration for garden center owner/operators is the development of supply chain management (SCM). The short definition is removing cost and time from the supply chain through lower inventories, electronic technology, and development of partnerships/alliances where information and its handling are important commodities.

In the mid-1980s, Wal-Mart experimented with what was then called a Quick Response Program, an SCM prototype, in some nonperishables categories. In the program, allies (other companies in the supply chain) were chosen; information was exchanged, with the results that the length of time from manufacture to sale was reduced dramatically. Cost saving occurred at many levels, including reduced inventories. The secret was not that business did not understand that inventories were costly, but they did not have the technology and organization to achieve the desired results. However, with scanning at checkout, upstream firms as partners rather than competitors, and demand better understood, manufacture and shipping could be coordinated. Wal-Mart reported that results exceeded their expectations, and they immediately looked for other applications and allies. As currently applied, SCM should reduce inventories, increase service levels, and build competitive advantage.

This concept was not the only reason for Wal-Mart's success, but the tremendous logistics advantage built since that time has been a very important contributing factor. SCM was applied across all categories of the store, including groceries. Wal-Mart moved from an insignificant player in the food market in the late 1980s to a sales leader today (Kurt Salmon Associates 1993). Grocery chains were looking for defensive strategies by the early 1990s, but they were already behind.

The situation in the ornamentals industry was similar to that described in the grocery industry. The mass merchandisers (big boxes) entered ornamentals retailing through their garden center categories earlier than groceries. They had a strategy of cost leadership, selling large volumes of standard product at low prices. The home center hardware stores entered in the mid-1980s. They found a different niche by competing a little less directly with Wal-Mart, and by incorporating a broader selection, a more knowledgeable staff, and perhaps somewhat better quality. Differentiation probably would best describe their strategy.

In the 1990s, SCM led to coordinated action through the supply chain. Activities of independent companies were coordinated to gain efficiencies similar to a single profit-maximizing entity (Ross 1999). Business began to see the contribution to efficiency from knowing customers' wants and needs from their own sales data, rather than from sales forecasts.

According to Hewitt (2001), "within a single enterprise, the performance improvement comes from better coordination of previously fragmented and discordant business practices in sales, warehousing, production, and so forth. Extend supply chain integration beyond the boundaries of an individual company by integrating processes and removing delays and redundancies among supply chain partners, and the results are even more impressive."

A significant business expense that has not been controlled is inventory. The holding of "safety stock" finished goods to avoid stockouts is rarely affordable. Inventory costs are more than the purchase price of the goods and include categories of opportunity costs, order costs, and holding costs (handling, obsolescence, damage, and other losses). Peter Drucker has argued that inventory of any kind, but particularly finished-goods inventory, is not an asset; it is a sunk cost. Every stock location adds significantly to operating costs.

SCM was considered after the point-of-sale information technology, the Universal Product Code, barcode scanning, and electronic data interchange (EDI) standards—along with computer hardware—became available. In the 1980s and 1990s, large amounts of real dollars and intellectual capital poured into business applications. Also, retailers had to understand that their sales information could be used to drive the system and reduce costs, and that sales/demand information had to be provided to others in the supply chain.

Finally, SCM is a relationship-based concept. Firms work together to identify the best ways to get product from manufacturer to store and customer. Partnerships/alliances form as a result. This is a newly adopted business model, in contrast to our traditional view of independent firms negotiating at arm's length for an advantage over upstream and downstream companies in the chain. In short, business had to overcome the anxiety of providing confidential information to other parties.

After these transformations, information from the barcode scanner at the front of the store could be used to drive the chain, from shelf space allocations and inventories at the store level, to when more product should be shipped to the store. This information can be accumulated over stores and similar procedures applied at the distribution center. Coordination with the manufacturer allows production according to need rather than according to a scheduled production run. With better knowledge of demand, inventories can be lower, and smaller shipments are feasible.

Over time, SCM came to be perceived as a source of competitive advantage. It has not remained a static concept and has drawn criticism. While touted as driven by consumer demand, analysts argue that many actual applications have stopped short of the retail outlet, because retailers hesitate to release sales data. Lee and Whang (2001) emphasize *demand* chain management (DCM) instead, where companies capture and use information to respond to actual customer demands quickly and accurately.

Collaborative forecasting, planning, and replenishment (CFPR) is a refinement to SCM in which technologies ensure that the right products are in the right places in the right quantities.

With appropriately designed production and logistics systems, companies can often use actual demand (direct pull) instead of forecast-based supply to drive materials flows at multiple points in the materials chain. And in an age when responsiveness and flexibility are key differentiators, it is clear that demand-driven operational processes will continue to gain ground over supply-driven ones in an ever-widening range of industries (Hewitt 2001).

The garden center sizes used as the basis of this work are not expected to adopt and implement SCM/CFPR directly. However, the concepts are extremely important, and management of our firms should be aware of these developments and should remain informed about advances in this area of the business. If they do not, the mass merchandisers who have incorporated these concepts and technologies will use this as an advantage to grow stronger. Mass merchandisers are very good at managing logistics and replenishment, and they have the resources to get better.

And, while direct adoption by these small garden centers of SCM/CFPR is not anticipated, there are other levels at which some of the advantages may be gained. Buying/exchange organizations are one example. Affiliation with associations like Home and Garden Showplace offer some of the advantages of buying as a group to gain market power as a buyer, and through selling promotion as well. There are options that allow smaller organizations to benefit from the concepts and technologies of SCM. Some third-party logistics (3PL) and channel management companies have invested in SCM/DCM technology and sell services to individual companies. This permits the costs to be spread over all the 3PL company's customers, and the small company benefits from the technological advances. Business-to-business (B2B) transactions are made more frequently through electronic exchanges that include bid and offer, and auction, approaches. Electronic technology applications are facilitated by emerging platforms that allow computers to speak with each other (Kinsey 2000). Data warehousing is a marketing option where data is purchased and used for very specific targeting of consumer groups within the market. Its advantage is to increase advertising and promotion efficiency by reducing mass marketing while increasing targeted marketing.

Implications for the Garden Center

Given these developments, how is competitive position analysis for small garden centers affected? They should be aware of the partnership relationships between producers and mass merchandisers. As these firms move closer in their alliances, their offer to other sellers may decline in quality, because a producer's important customers are likely to get the better product. The mass merchandisers require that producers who sell to them upgrade in terms of electronic technology for demand/supply chain management. If the producer is reliable in terms of deliveries and quality, the relationship can be long-lasting and profitable for the grower. However, mass merchandisers have become more demanding in other ways. They ask growers to provide an expanding set of services. Frequent deliveries (which helps solve problems such as untrained and inattentive "associates") is one of those areas. Additional equipment such as rolling trays, assistance in unloading the truck, assistance in placing stock in sales areas, and some expertise in management of the category—these are areas where mass merchandisers expect assistance from their suppliers.

The result is lower cost and an increasing level of competitiveness by mass merchandisers. Pressure on the profitability of the garden center component of retailing, which has been losing market share nationally, increases. The conclusion that garden centers will not compete with mass merchandisers on a cost basis, except in some very unusual circumstances, seems clear. The importance of competitive analysis—being properly positioned in the market from the start—rises.

Good strategies arise from general trends that describe consumers. While the importance of these trends varies (by region of the country, for example), they provide a beginning point for analysis. Consumers are older, richer, wiser, and busier; hence, environmental awareness, the large seniors' market, the baby boomlet, the pace of urban life, and the shrinking nuclear family all offer opportunities. In addition, some leaders in market analysis argue that the necessary analysis has passed from demographics into the realm of psychographics (Feather 1990). This distinction contrasts the study of income, race, sex, and other similar factors with the determination of the psychological perceptions, wants, and needs of customers.

Other factors are influenced by choice of strategy and location. When a site is chosen, many characteristics and directions of the firm are set. A garden center might be close to a large population center, located near an upper-middle-class residential district, along a major road with high traffic, easily accessible, and surrounded by compatible businesses. These factors could help attract customers and reduce promotional expenses. A less desirable location might be purchased at far less initial expense, but promotional expenditures plus price concessions would often be required to compensate for the poorer location.

SITE CONSIDERATIONS AND PLANNING

Before a single dollar is spent, the owner must develop a comprehensive plan for the site. Figure 1 (page 12) presents a checklist of questions to ask before purchasing a property for a garden center or expanding an existing center. The checklist is an enumeration of requirements for the facility. By answering the questions, the garden center operator can develop a garden center "program" (Wertheim 1991). When planning, the garden center operator should think in terms of at least a ten-year horizon. Once the master plan is completed and a preliminary cost established, attention should be paid to how the project can be phased, depending on resource availability and budgetary constraints. Phasing must be done very carefully, because the first phase may not attract sufficient numbers of the customers the owner has targeted.

CAPITAL INVESTMENT

As indicated earlier, two model firms were developed to represent typical garden center characteristics for two sizes of firms (tables 2 and 3, pages 13 and 15). In order to create workable models, each firm is assumed to be a garden center whose sole activity is the retail sale of plants and supplies. In reality, garden centers may include a variety of related businesses, such as nursery production, landscape installation, or landscape maintenance.

The competitive forces and generic strategies discussed earlier (see "Starting a Business," page 3) support the alternative garden center sizes selected for this study. The larger garden center (garden center A), with sales of $1 million, is large enough to gain some economies of size and scale, may be too small to compete with the mass merchandisers and large garden centers, and might adopt a differentiation strategy. The smaller garden center (garden center B), with sales of $350,000, is assumed to have a focus strategy. It is located in an area with less competition, specializes on the needs of the local community, and attempts to hold down costs through less expensive physical facilities.

Land

The cost of land varies dramatically throughout the United States. It is often necessary to compromise between a desirable and an affordable location. The operator should select the best location he or she can afford, because it is very difficult to change locations once established.

Layouts have been designed for garden centers A and B (figures 2 and 3, pages 17 and 18). These layouts represent the capital investment decisions made for each garden center and were necessary to provide data for determining costs. While design principles have been followed, **the layouts are not intended as blueprints for a finished garden center.** A garden center must be designed to meet the needs and characteristics of individual site and business circumstances. Local zoning ordinances and building codes will also influence each garden center layout.

Garden Center A:

Garden center A is located on four acres of unimproved land. The lot is 312 feet by 558 feet. Three hundred feet is a minimum amount of frontage required to allow cars to enter and exit conveniently. This lot costs $1,282 per frontage foot ($100,000 per acre) for a total cost of approximately $400,000.

Garden Center B:

Garden center B is located on two acres (312 feet by 280 feet) of unimproved land. For the smaller market area, land costs are $641 per frontage foot, or $100,000 per acre, for a total cost of approximately

Figure 1. Selected basic questions to be answered prior to buying property for a garden center

1. What is the market area? Can it support a garden center?
2. What are the plans of community development for the next five years for this location?
3. What is the income distribution of the community?
4. What is the age group?
5. How much grading needs to be done?
6. How easy is it to get onto the property or leave the property?
7. What is the automobile count per day?
8. How does the site drain? Is a retention pond required? Are there provisions for pollution control?
9. Are sewer, water, natural gas, electrical, and telephone adjacent to the site?
10. If only using septic tanks, what is the perc test?
11. Is well water going to be used? What is the quality of the water? How many gallons will it produce per minute? Will a storage tank be required?
12. What are the fire marshal's requirements for water storage, access road, building sprinklers, fireproof roof?
13. What is the cost of bringing utilities to the building site?
14. Have you studied the Zoning Code? Do you have the correct zoning for operating a garden center? What are the conditions for a land-use permit?
15. Do you need deer protection?
16. Has anyone conducted a soil-engineering test?
17. What do you wish to build? (Think in terms of 10 years, minimum.)
    a. Parking area–how many customer cars, employee spaces, and company vehicles?
    b. Do you need a perimeter road?
    c. How much landscaping do you wish to do? Are there any landscape requirements? What are the landscape maintenance costs?
    d. What are the sign ordinances?
    e. What size should the store be?
    f. What size for the tropical house?
    g. How much storage area or warehouse is needed?
    h. What size outdoor sales area?
    i. How much shade area is required?
    j. How much area is required for bagged goods?
    k. Will you sell anything in bulk and, if so, what size bins and how many? Do you need a scale for weighing trucks?
    l. What size plant receiving and staging area will you need?
    m. How large a space is needed for the area where customer deliveries will be temporarily stored?
    n. How do you plan to protect bedding plants in spring? How many tables do you require?
    o. What type of merchandise do you plan to sell in the store?
    p. How many restrooms will you need?
    q. What size lunchroom, janitor's closet, label-making room, and similar rooms will be required?
    r. How many offices are required and what size?
    s. What interior and exterior fixtures will you need?
    t. Do you need a Christmas storage area?
    u. What kind of a security system will you need?
    v. What kind of a telephone system do you need? What kind of an intercom? Will you have radios?
    w. Are you planning to have a gift shop, produce shop, landscape design service, florist, or similar areas?
18. Have you established a budget for construction?
19. Have you established a budget for architects and consultants?
20. What is the timetable for planning? What is the timetable for building, and how much time is allowed to move in and get ready for operation?
21. How are you going to finance the project?
22. Is there good reason to anticipate that property value will increase, and therefore buying this property would be a good investment?

Source: Ernest Wertheim; Wertheim, van der Ploeg, and Klemeyer; 1989.

Table 2. Capital requirements for garden center A with annual sales of $1,000,000, 1991

ITEM	DESCRIPTION	UNIT	QUANTITY	COST/UNIT	TOTAL COST
LAND					
Unimproved land	Urban area, highway frontage, flat	Front footage	312	$1,282.05	$400,000
Improvements	Clearing, grading, drainage, gravel [a]	Acre	4	25,000.00	100,000
Parking lot	Asphalt 3-1/2" w/8" stone base [b]	Sq. ft.	31,280	1.66	51,925
Parking bumpers	Concrete	Spaces	66	20.19	1,333
Security fence	Chain link, 7-1/2', two sides and back	Linear ft.	1,428	16.07	22,948
Security chain	Two posts w/chain across drive	Each	3	150.00	450
Sign	Roadside	Each	1	5,000.00	5,000
Security lights	Aluminum, three-arm pole	Each	6	2,000.00	12,000
Loading area	Asphalt 4" w/8" stone base [b]	Sq. ft.	2,850	1.80	5,130
Service road	Asphalt 3" w/4" stone base	Sq. ft.	22,520	1.66	37,383
Graveled display	Gravel 4"	Sq. ft.	12,192	– [b]	– [b]
Display beds	Landscape ties [c]	Each	720	12.79	9,209
Irrigation	Overhead container, drip B & B [d]	System	1	8,000.00	8,000
Landscaping		Sq. ft.	11,000	1.25	13,750
TOTAL LAND AND IMPROVEMENTS					**$667,128**
BUILDINGS					
Sales building [e]	Metal, drywall, heated and AC	Sq. ft.	6,000	32.00	192,000
Greenhouse and work area	Two gutter-connected, acrylic, concrete floor	Sq. ft.	4,000	10.50	42,000
Overwintering greenhouse	20' x 100' poly quonset	Each	4	2,000.00	8,000
Lath shade	Gravel floor, wooden lath	Sq. ft.	10,500	0.62	6,510
Pole barn	20' x 50'	Sq. ft.	1,000	8.50	8,500
Bulk bins and apron	4-10' x 10' bulk materials storage [f]	Each	1	3,985.00	3,985
Interior display shelves	Allowance			5,000.00	5,000
Cashier counters	Allowance	Each	4	500.00	2,000
Gazebo	Allowance	Each	1	5,000.00	5,000
Benches	4' x 8' covered hardware cloth [g]	Each	24	75.00	1,800
Wooden display spools [h]					–
Information center	Information kiosk	Sq. ft.	25	12.00	300
TOTAL BUILDINGS					**275,095**
TOTAL LAND AND BUILDINGS					**942,223**
EQUIPMENT					
Office equipment	Computer, copier, furniture, etc. [i]	System			$12,000
Pickup truck	Fully equipped	Each	1	$15,000.00	15,000
Truck	Stake body w/dump	Each	1	20,000.00	20,000
Skid loader	Adapted	Each	1	25,000.00	25,000
Water cooler		Each	1	370.00	370
Fire extinguishers		Each	4	140.00	560
Cash registers		Each	4	500.00	2,000
Credit card scanners		Each	4	460.00	1,840
Scales		Each	1	50.00	50

(Continued on next page)

Table 2. Capital requirements for garden center A with annual sales of $1,000,000, 1991 ***(continued from previous page)***

ITEM	DESCRIPTION	UNIT	QUANTITY	COST/UNIT	TOTAL COST
EQUIPMENT					
Customer wagons		Each	45	90.00	4,050
Utility nursery carts		Each	5	200.00	1,000
Tree dollies		Each	2	200.00	400
Hand trucks	Two wheels	Each	2	250.00	500
Wheelbarrows		Each	4	100.00	400
Sprayers	Backpack	Each	2	100.00	200
Sprayer	Hand pump	Each	1	40.00	40
Proportioner	For liquid fertilizer	Each	1	200.00	200
Drop spreader	For fertilizing landscape	Each	1	45.00	45
Lawn mower		Each	1	250.00	250
Hand tools	Shovels, rakes, shears, etc.	System		800.00	800
Water hoses	75' for hand watering	Each	25	15.00	375
Watering wands	For hand watering	Each	10	10.00	100
Signs	Throughout garden center [j]	System		3,000.00	3,000
TOTAL EQUIPMENT					**88,180**
GRAND TOTAL [k]					**$1,030,403**

Note: The numbers used for start-up costs and financial statements in this book are for illustration purposes only. They are not intended to reflect accurate estimates of the costs associated with establishing and operating a garden center. Garden center operators should use the charts and tables as guidelines for entering their own numbers to accurately reflect their own true costs.

[a] *All area except buildings and asphalted areas graveled 4" deep*
[b] *See footnote a, another 4" of crushed stone added to initial 4" base*
[c] *Timbers 6" x 6" x 6' pressure-treated*
[d] *Plus landscaping; entire system on timers*
[e] *Display, offices, storage, and two restrooms*
[f] *Concrete base plus 10'-wide concrete apron*
[g] *Pressure-treated 2" x 4" frame on two saw horses*
[h] *Spools are usually free but some pickup cost may be incurred*
[i] *See appendix table A (page 57) for details of office equipment and furniture*
[j] *Durable signs and sign holders*
[k] *Assume that items such as utility deposits, building permits, sales taxes, etc., are included*

Table 3. Capital requirements for garden center B with annual sales of $350,000, 1991

ITEM	DESCRIPTION	UNIT	QUANTITY	COST/UNIT	TOTAL COST
LAND					
Unimproved land	Suburban, highway frontage, flat	Front footage	312	$ 641.02	$200,000
Improvements	Clearing, grading, draining, graveling [a/]	Acre	2	25,000.00	50,000
Parking lot and service road	8" crushed stone [b/]	Sq. ft.	11,384	0.62	7,058
Parking bumpers	Concrete	Each	18	20.19	363
Security chain	Two posts w/chain across drive	Each	1	150.00	150
Display beds	Landscape ties [c/]	Each	525	12.79	6,715
Sign	Roadside	Each	1	1,000.00	1,000
Landscaping	Edge of parking lot	Sq. ft.	3,250	1.25	4,062
Security lights	Aluminum, three-arm pole	Each	2	2,000.00	4,000
Irrigation	Overhead	System	1	3,500.00	3,500
TOTAL LAND AND IMPROVEMENTS					**276,848**
BUILDINGS					
Sales building [d/]	Drywall with concrete floor	Sq. ft.	1,080	35.00	37,800
Storage building	8' x 12'	Sq. ft.	96	5.21	500
Greenhouse	20' x 100' poly quonset [e/]	Sq. ft.	2,000	4.00	8,000
Enclosed walkway	Connects sales and greenhouse	Sq. ft.	20	15.00	300
Work area	Concrete floor work area in greenhouse	Sq. ft.	200	2.50	500
Overwintering greenhouses	20' x 100' poly quonset	Each	2	2,000.00	4,000
Lath	Gravel floor, wooden lath	Sq. ft.	1,992	0.62	1,235
Benches	4'x 8' covered hardware cloth [f/]	Each	14	75.00	1,050
Wooden display spools [g/]					–
Interior display shelves	Allowance			1,000.00	1,000
Cashier counter	Allowance	Each	1	500.00	500
TOTAL BUILDINGS					**54,885**
TOTAL LAND AND BUILDINGS					**331,733**
EQUIPMENT					
Pickup truck		Each	1	$15,000.00	$ 15,000
Office furniture		System		1,050.00	1,050
Fire extinguisher		Each	1	140.00	140
Scale		Each	1	50.00	50
Water cooler		Each	1	370.00	370
Cash register		Each	1	500.00	500
Credit card scanner		Each	1	460.00	460
Hand tools	Shovels, rakes, shears, etc.	System		300.00	300
Wheelbarrows		Each	2	100.00	200
Drop spreader	For fertilizing landscape	Each	1	45.00	45
Sprayers	Backpack	Each	2	100.00	200
Tree dolly		Each	1	200.00	200
Lawn mower		Each	1	250.00	250
Utility nursery carts		Each	1	200.00	200
Customer wagon		Each	12	90.00	1,080

(Continued on next page)

Table 3. Capital requirements for garden center B with annual sales of $350,000, 1991 *(continued from previous page)*

ITEM	DESCRIPTION	UNIT	QUANTITY	COST/UNIT	TOTAL COST
EQUIPMENT					
Proportioner	For liquid fertilizing	Each	1	200.00	200
Water hose	75' for hand watering	Each	10	15.00	150
Watering wand	For hand watering	Each	5	10.00	50
Signs	Throughout garden center [h/]	System		1,000.00	1,000
TOTAL EQUIPMENT					**21,445**
GRAND TOTAL [i/]					**$ 353,178**

Note: The numbers used for start-up costs and financial statements in this book are for illustration purposes only. They are not intended to reflect accurate estimates of the costs associated with establishing and operating a garden center. Garden center operators should use the charts and tables as guidelines for entering their own numbers to accurately reflect their own true costs.

[a/] *All area except sales building graveled 4" deep*
[b/] *Another 4" of crushed stone added to the initial 4" base*
[c/] *Timbers 6" x 6" x 6' pressure-treated*
[d/] *Display, one restroom, offices, heated and AC*
[e/] *Heated, fan-cooled, gravel floor, saran*
[f/] *Pressure-treated 2" x 4" frame on two saw horses*
[g/] *Spools are usually free but some pickup cost may be incurred*
[h/] *Durable signs and sign holders*
[i/] *Assumes that items such as utility deposits, building permits, sales taxes, etc., are included*

Figure 2. Layout of garden center A

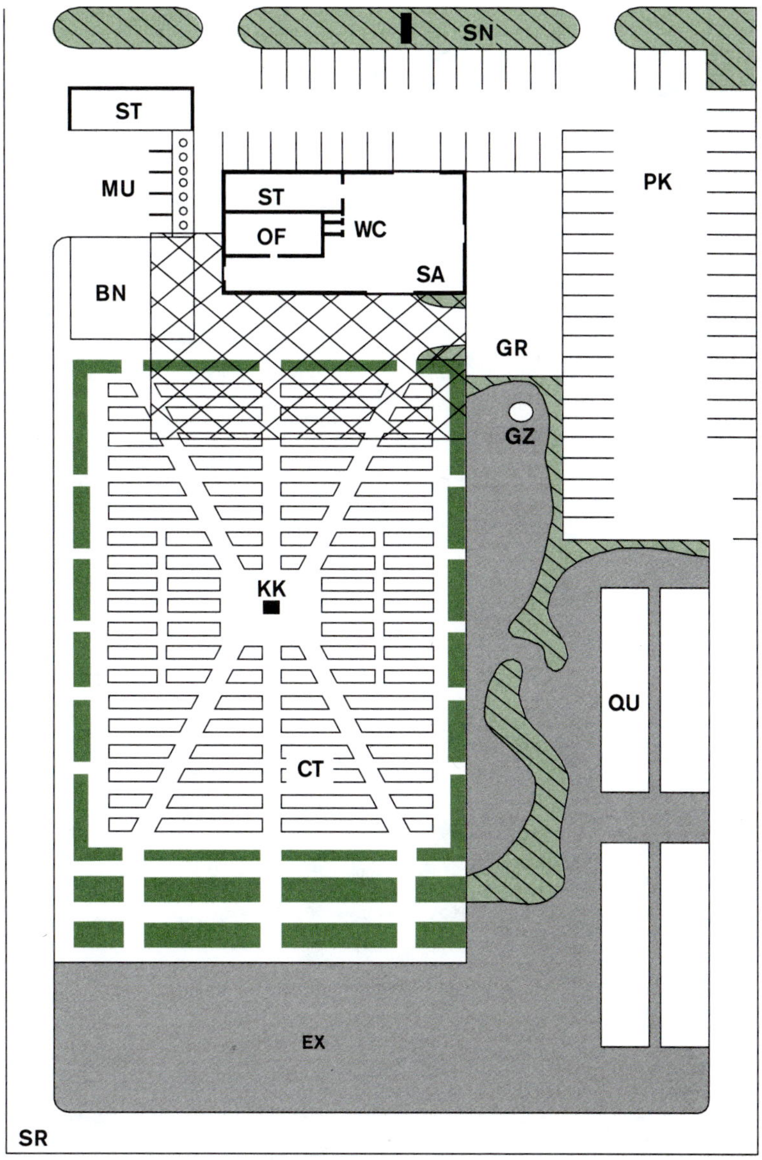

	Display Beds – Trees		Landscaping	EX	Expansion Area
	Lath		Hard Good Display	GR	Greenhouse
SN	Sign	WC	Restrooms	GZ	Gazebo
PK	Parking	BN	Display Bench	MU	Mulch
ST	Storage	CT	Container Display Blocks	KK	Kiosk
SA	Sales Room	SR	Service Road	OF	Office Complex
		QU	Overwintering Quonset		

Figure 3. Layout of garden center B

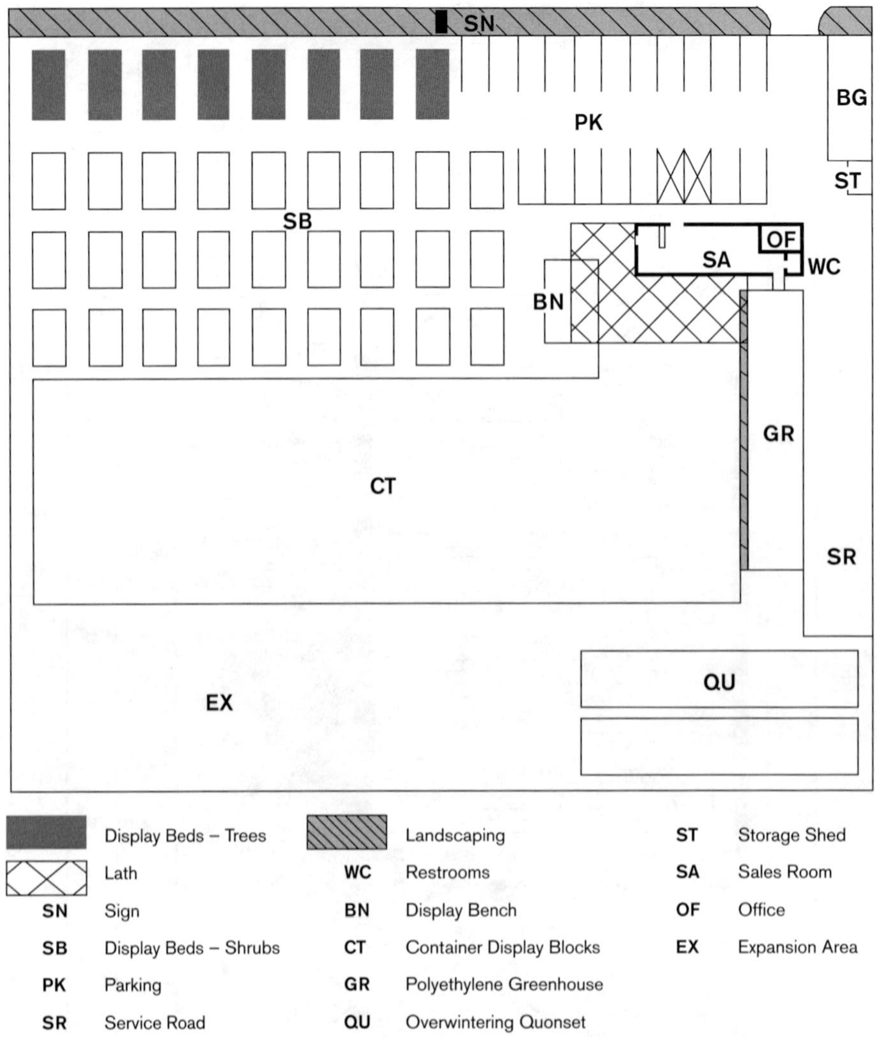

$200,000. The two modeled garden centers have identical frontage, but the lot depths vary.

Land Improvements

Land improvements vary with the condition of the land and utilities available. Improvements may include clearing, grading, drainage (retention pond), well or municipal water hook-up, sewer hook-up, or septic system. Inclusion of a retention pond may be dictated by environmental conditions and runoff regulations in the future. A figure of $25,000 per acre is included for land preparation. This figure includes a four-inch layer of gravel spread over the site (excluding paved areas and building locations). Other utilities including electric and gas services should be considered. These costs will vary depending on the equipment needed and local regulations.

Parking Lot

The size of the parking lot affects customer turnover in the garden center. Parking lots should be designed to hold the number of cars expected during peak usage (weekends and/or spring months). A rule of thumb is to allow 400 square feet per car with an additional 10% for landscaped traffic islands. Depending on the site and configuration of the parking lot, this may not be possible. Spaces should be lined in some manner to increase parking efficiency. Though paving is more desirable, a less expensive alternative is a gravel parking lot. In gravel lots, parking space bumpers must be used to park cars efficiently.

The entrance to the parking lot should be clear and should not create a traffic hazard. Landscaping can help improve the appearance of the parking lot and demonstrate mature landscape plants as an example of how plants can be used in the landscape.

Garden Center A:
A paved and lined parking lot will offer convenience and encourage efficient parking. A 31,280-square-foot (66-space) paved parking lot has been specified for garden center A.

Paving is also included for 1,500 square feet to be used for vehicular traffic and as a loading area. A 20-foot-wide service road establishes the perimeter of garden center A. The service road allows for easy access to all parts of the garden center. Trucks can be unloaded close to the display beds and storage areas.

Garden Center B:
Garden center B has 18 parking spaces in a 6,600-square-foot gravel lot.

Security

Security can be handled in a variety of ways. The best choice will depend on zoning regulations and the uses of surrounding properties. In some situations, a chain across the entrance is sufficient. Other situations require a security fence, and some zoning laws may require an attractive screening fence. Lights can be used to increase security as well as provide for night sales.

Garden Center A:
A six-foot chain-link fence encompasses three sides of the property in garden center A. Three chains are used at the entrances to the parking lot. Six 30-foot aluminum three-arm light poles provide additional security.

Garden Center B:
In garden center B, a chain across the entrance to the parking lot and two 30-foot aluminum three-arm light poles are used for security.

Buildings

The buildings in a garden center function to provide display space for hard goods and plant materials, office space, storage, and overwintering facilities.

Sales Building

The sales building is an area for indoor display of merchandise. The sales building might also house offices, meeting rooms, restrooms, and indoor storage. The entrance to the sales room should be well-marked and attractive.

The sales room should be organized to create a traffic pattern that encourages customers to visit all displays. Approximately 30% of the space should be devoted to display.

The number of checkouts required for a garden center can be calculated by dividing the dollar volume per day at a peak sales time by the capacity of a typical cashier (approximately $8,000 per day). An 8-by-12-foot area is required for each checkout line.

Garden Center A:
In garden center A, the sales building is a metal frame building with a concrete floor and interior drywall. It is ventilated, heated, and air-conditioned. The sales building includes a 4,080-square-foot sales room; 1,000-square-foot storage room; 840 square feet of office space; and two restrooms (80 square feet). The office space is divided into four rooms—

owner's office, computer room, work station, and break room (table 4).

Four cash registers are planned, one being mobile for placement during peak sales along the path exiting from displays to the parking lot. The other three checkouts are in the sales building. An allowance of $7,000 has been provided for the cashier counters and interior display shelves in garden center A.

Garden Center B:

In garden center B, the sales building is a wood frame building with a concrete floor and interior drywall. It is heated, ventilated, and air-conditioned. The building (1,078 square feet) includes a sales room (880 square feet), office (150 square feet), and one restroom (48 square feet). Within the 150 square feet of office space for garden center B is an allocation for one desk, two chairs, two filing cabinets, and one metal bookshelf.

One cash register is required for garden center B. The allowance for the cashier counter and interior display shelves is $1,500.

Display Greenhouse

A display greenhouse is an important component of the garden center. It helps extend the season by providing an area for the display of indoor plants and provides a pleasant place to shop in inclement weather. The display greenhouse should be attached to the sales building or connected via a covered walkway to encourage customer traffic through the greenhouse and extend the interior display space.

A display greenhouse is very different from a production greenhouse. In a production house, every possible square foot is used for production space. A display house must be arranged attractively to promote leisurely traffic flow throughout the space. Modular display tables, such as cable, phone, or electricity wire spools, are an inexpensive (often free) way to create a free-form display.

Garden Center A:

In garden center A, a 4,000-square-foot, gutter-connected acrylic greenhouse is attached to the sales building. The greenhouse is heated and ventilated. A four-inch layer of concrete is used for the floor to make wagon and cart use convenient. A 200-square-foot section of the house is screened from the public and used as a work area.

Garden Center B:

In garden center B, the greenhouse is a 2,000-square-foot, heated, and ventilated poly quonset house. The greenhouse is located five feet from the sales building and connected by an enclosed walkway. The greenhouse floor is gravel.

Overwintering Houses

Plants are overwintered in both garden centers in 20-by-100-foot unheated poly quonset

Table 4. Configuration of office space for garden center A

OWNER'S OFFICE	COMPUTER ROOM	WORK STATION	BREAK ROOM
120 sq. ft.	120 sq. ft.	300 sq. ft.	300 sq. ft.
1 desk	1 desk	Flat table	2 6-ft. tables
2 chairs	2 chairs	Drafting table	12 chairs
2 file cabinets	2 file cabinets	2 chairs	
Metal bookshelf	Metal bookshelf	Stool	
Computer	Large metal cabinet		
Printer	Desktop copier		
Fax machine	Laminator		

overwintering houses. For information about overwintering practices and structures, see *Principles, Practices, and Comparative Costs of Overwintering Container-Grown Landscape Plants* (Southern Cooperative Series Bulletin 313, The Pennsylvania State University, May 1986).

Garden Centers A and B:
Four overwintering houses are specified for garden center A, while two are specified for garden center B.

Storage

Space for storage may be included in the sales building or made available in a variety of separate facilities.

Garden Center A:
In garden center A, a 12-foot-high pole barn, enclosed on three sides, with metal siding and a concrete floor is used for storage and display of bagged hard goods. Bulk goods, such as mulch, sand, and stone are stored in bulk material storage bins. The storage building and bins have been positioned to allow dump truck access for unloading.

Garden Center B:
An outdoor shed (100 square feet) is used for storage in garden center B.

Outdoor Sales Area

The outdoor sales area consists of overhead lath, display tables, display beds (for balled and burlapped plants) and display blocks (for container plants). Factors affecting the choice of surface for the outdoor sales area include comfort, cost, convenience, flexibility, and impact on plant quality. While concrete and asphalt provide a comfortable and convenient surface for foot and cart traffic, they are expensive and provide a poor surface for the display of plant material. Gravel is less expensive and provides a good surface for plant display. Unfortunately, it is uncomfortable for walking and inconvenient for carts. One solution is to use gravel for beds and concrete for walkways. But, once implemented, the layout of the garden center is permanent.

Walks in the outdoor sales area should be 12 feet, eight feet, or six feet wide. A convenient size for beds used for the display of small trees is 12 feet wide (the width of four trees). Shrub beds and blocks should be six feet wide. This width makes efficient use of the ratio between walk and display space and allows customers to reach each plant easily.

A lath area is used for displaying hanging baskets and shade-loving bedding plants, perennials, and woody ornamentals. Lath provides comfort for the customer as well as shade for the plants.

A highlight such as a gazebo, water feature, specimen plant, or demonstration garden can be located within 75 feet of the sales room door. A gazebo placed in the outdoor sales area will provide a focal point, draw customers out of the sales building, and give them a place to relax in a pleasant, landscaped environment.

Garden Center A:
In garden center A, open areas in the outdoor sales area are paved with two-inch asphalt. Display blocks and walkways are covered with a four-inch layer of gravel provided during site preparation.

Display beds for balled and burlapped (B&B) or large-container materials are three landscape ties high, filled with soil, and topped with mulch. The four-inch gravel used in site preparation serves as the foundation for display of container materials. Drip irrigation is installed in the eight large tree display beds. The rest of the outdoor sales area is watered with overhead irrigation and hand-held hoses. Hose bibs are located in the display area 75 to 100 feet on centers.

The display tables are designed for bedding plant and perennial display. Each table is four feet by eight feet. Hardware cloth is attached to two-by-four-inch pressure-treated lumber, while two sawhorses support each table. Other options include tables on cinder blocks or custom-built tiered benches.

The lath area covers a portion of the display tables, display beds, and display blocks. A gazebo acts as the highlight to draw customers into the outdoor sales area.

An information kiosk is located in the center of the outdoor sales area. The kiosk will be staffed by a trained horticulturist, who will answer technical questions from customers. Additional salespeople will circulate throughout the sales area.

Garden Center B:
In garden center B, the outdoor sales area is covered with four inches of gravel (provided during site preparation). Display beds for balled and burlapped (B&B) or large-container materials are three landscape ties high, filled with soil, and topped with mulch. The outdoor sales area is watered with a combination of overhead irrigation and hand-held hoses. Hose bibs are located in the display area 75 to 100 feet on centers.

Display tables are as specified in garden center A. Lath covers display tables, display blocks, and an open display area.

> ### *HANDICAP ACCESS*
>
> *When designing the garden center, an important consideration is handicap access. Consideration for handicapped customers will affect parking, entrances, grade changes (use ramps), and bathrooms. Federal, state, or local ordinances may make this mandatory.*

Vehicles and Equipment

Trucks are used by a garden center for the pickup and delivery of plant material. A stake body truck with a dump bed can be used to deliver mulch, stone, sand, or any other bulk good. Bulk materials can be moved around in the garden center with a skid loader adapted with a bucket. A steel frame for the skid loader is useful for moving palletized container plants and bagged hard goods. Many garden centers have access to additional equipment if they are associated with a landscape business.

Garden Center A:
Garden center A is equipped with the following vehicles and large equipment: a pickup truck, a stake body truck with dump bed, and an adapted skid loader with a bucket and steel frame for pallets. Additional indoor and outdoor equipment is detailed in table 2 (page 13).

Garden Center B:
Garden center B is equipped with a pickup truck. Additional indoor and outdoor equipment is detailed in table 3 (page 15).

PRODUCT MIX AND TURNOVER

Each garden center must carefully appraise and select products and services to be included in the product mix. Product mix includes product lines, plant species and cultivars, variations of sizes, variations of quality, and services offered. Product mix is selected to meet the wants and needs of the market and to fit the image of the garden center.

As a garden center increases in size and diversity, a greater percentage of the product mix will be hard goods and gift items (table 5).

Garden center A was assumed to be much more involved with nonplant sales than garden center B (table 5). Garden center A has gift items and a Christmas shop but no patio furniture. Garden center B was assumed to handle the more basic hard goods such as potting media, fertilizer, and pesticides.

The annual turnover for the alternative firm sizes was designed to be essentially the same except that garden center A had a higher turnover of container trees and shrubs (table 5). For purposes of estimating inventory, a weighted annual average turnover (product mix percentage x annual turnover) was calculated for each garden center.

In order to ascertain cost of goods, an estimate of gross margins was necessary for each category of items in the product mix. The gross margin was calculated the same for each garden center. Gross margin ranged from a low of 40% for hard goods to 75% for balled and burlapped (B&B) trees and shrubs.

FINANCIAL STATEMENTS

Financial information is presented for the two representative garden centers based on specific operating assumptions. The two major financial documents to consider are the income statement and the balance sheet. These forms help businesses organize financial information for tax preparation and ratio calculation. The ratios are used as diagnostic tools to assess the strengths and weaknesses of a company; as indicators of progress to chart company growth; and as tools for future planning. (A detailed discussion follows in the "Financial Analysis" section, page 52.)

Table 5. Product turnover for two selected garden centers, 1991

MERCHANDISE	PERCENTAGE PRODUCT MIX	ANNUAL TURNOVER	WEIGHTED AVERAGE ANNUAL TURNOVER
GARDEN CENTER A:			
Balled and burlapped trees and shrubs	9	1.2	0.11
Container trees and shrubs	26	7.0	1.82
Bedding plants and perennials	11	9.0	0.99
Other plants [a]	15	4.0	0.60
Hard goods [b]	39	3.0	1.17
TOTAL	**100**	–	**4.69**
GARDEN CENTER B:			
Balled and burlapped trees and shrubs	10	1.2	0.12
Container trees and shrubs	30	5.0	1.50
Bedding plants and perennials	17	9.0	1.53
Other plants [a]	15	4.0	0.60
Hard goods [b]	28	3.0	0.84
TOTAL	**100**		**4.59**

[a] *Includes foliage plants, seasonal potted plants, hanging baskets, seeds, and bulbs*
[b] *Includes fertilizers, pesticides, media (potting, mulch, sand, and gravel), tools, garden ornaments, gift items, pottery and ceramic pots, Christmas shop, and miscellaneous hard goods*

Income Statement

The average percentage cost of goods was obtained by multiplying the individual percentage cost of goods items by the appropriate percentage of product mix (table 6). This resulted in an estimated cost of goods of 47.23% for garden center A and of 45.20% for garden center B. However, these data assume that the desired gross margin is achieved. This relationship is not realized because merchandise losses, damaged merchandise, volume discounts, and markdowns for sales reduce the margin achieved. Therefore, the average cost of goods estimates were increased by 5% to adjust for these deviations. In some cases, the 5% adjustment will be low relative to actual experience. If extensive markdowns will be used, initial markups should be higher, or the targeted gross profits will not be achieved.

To illustrate the potential profits from the garden centers, pro forma income statements were derived (tables 7 and 8). A new garden center could not open for business and achieve its designed level of capacity in sales in the first year or two, a consideration when interpreting the pro forma income statements.

Payroll taxes and so forth were assumed to be 20% of total salary costs. If the business is incorporated, the owner-manager's salary is considered as an expense as shown in tables 7 and 8. If the business is not incorporated, the funds taken from the

Table 6. Initial cost of goods calculation for two selected garden centers, 1991

MERCHANDISE	PRODUCT MIX PERCENTAGE	GROSS MARGIN PERCENTAGE	COST OF GOOD PERCENT [a]	PERCENT OF TOTAL SALES [b]
GARDEN CENTER A:				
Balled and burlapped trees and shrubs	9	75	25	2.25
Container trees and shrubs	26	67	33	8.58
Bedding plants and perennials	11	50	50	5.50
Other plant materials [c]	15	50	50	7.50
Hard goods [d]	39	40	60	23.40
TOTAL	**100**	–	–	**47.23**
ADJUSTED COST OF GOODS [e]	–	–	–	**49.59**
GARDEN CENTER B:				
Balled and burlapped trees and shrubs	10	75	25	2.50
Container trees and shrubs	30	67	33	9.90
Bedding plants and perennials	17	50	50	8.50
Other plant materials [c]	15	50	50	7.50
Hard goods [d]	28	40	60	16.80
TOTAL	**100**	–	–	**45.20**
ADJUSTED COST OF GOODS [e]	–	–	–	**47.46**

[a] *100 minus markup (gross margin) percentage*

[b] *Cost of good percentage times product mix*

[c] *Includes foliage plants, seasonal potted plants, hanging baskets, seeds, sod, and bulbs*

[d] *Includes fertilizers, pesticides, media (potting, mulch, sand, and gravel), tools, garden ornaments, gift items, pottery and ceramic pots, Christmas shop, and miscellaneous hard goods*

[e] *The total cost of goods percentage assumes full markup on all merchandise and that it sells for the marked price. This is not achieved because of merchandise losses, damaged merchandise, volume discounts, and markdowns for sales. Therefore, the total cost of goods was increased by 5% in order to achieve the targeted sales volume.*

business by the owner-manager for his/her contribution are not considered as a business expense, but rather profit would be increased by this amount. Withdrawals would reduce contributions equity as shown in the net worth statement and on the balance sheet. Other items, except depreciation, were derived with the assistance of survey data and garden center operating cost studies. These items were generally estimated as percentages of sales. The items could be expected to vary considerably by business organization and location. Property taxes, insurance rates, advertising rates, and utilities will vary widely with location. Advertising was placed

Table 7. Pro forma income statement for garden center A ($1,000,000 in sales), 2001

ITEMS	DOLLARS ($)	PERCENT OF SALES (%)
Sales	1,000,000	100.0
Cost of goods [a]	496,000	49.6
Gross profit	504,000	50.4
EXPENSES:		
Management/owner salaries	50,000	5.0
Employee salaries	180,000	18.0
Payroll taxes, etc. (20%)	46,000	4.6
Property taxes	20,000	2.0
Insurance on buildings, equipment, inventory	20,000	2.0
Advertising	30,000	3.0
Depreciation [b]	50,080	5.0
Utilities	20,000	2.0
Repairs and maintenance [c]	10,000	1.0
Office and operating supplies [d]	15,000	1.5
Vehicle expenses	10,000	1.0
Legal, accounting, auditing	5,000	0.5
Bank charges and credit card discounts	3,000	0.3
Dues, donations, subscriptions	2,000	0.2
Travel, conventions, entertainment	2,000	0.2
Miscellaneous expenses [e]	10,000	1.0
TOTAL EXPENSES	**473,080**	**47.3**
NET PROFIT BEFORE TAXES	**30,920**	**3.1**

Note: The numbers used for start-up costs and financial statements in this book are for illustration purposes only. They are not intended to reflect accurate estimates of the costs associated with establishing and operating a garden center. Garden center operators should use the charts and tables as guidelines for entering their own numbers to accurately reflect their own true costs.

a/ *See table 6, page 24*
b/ *See appendix tables A, B, and C (pages 57–61) for details of depreciation calculations*
c/ *Includes mulching plants in display beds*
d/ *Includes expendable sign materials*
e/ *Includes liability insurance*

Table 8. Pro forma income statement for garden center B ($350,000 in sales), 2001

ITEMS	DOLLARS ($)	PERCENT OF SALES (%)
Sales	350,000	100.0
Cost of goods [a]	166,110	47.5
Gross profit	183,890	52.5
EXPENSES:		
Management/owner salaries	30,000	8.6
Employee salaries	65,000	18.6
Payroll taxes, etc. (20%)	19,000	5.4
Property taxes	3,500	1.0
Insurance on buildings, equipment, inventory	3,500	1.0
Advertising	10,500	3.0
Depreciation [b]	10,947	3.1
Utilities	5,250	1.5
Repairs and maintenance [c]	2,800	0.8
Office and operating supplies [d]	5,250	1.5
Vehicle expenses	3,500	1.0
Legal, accounting, auditing	1,750	0.5
Bank charges and credit card discounts	1,050	0.3
Dues, donations, subscriptions	700	0.2
Travel, conventions, entertainment	700	0.2
Miscellaneous expenses [e]	3,500	1.0
TOTAL EXPENSES	**166,947**	**47.7**
NET PROFIT BEFORE TAXES	**16,943**	**4.8**

Note: The numbers used for start-up costs and financial statements in this book are for illustration purposes only. They are not intended to reflect accurate estimates of the costs associated with establishing and operating a garden center. Garden center operators should use the charts and tables as guidelines for entering their own numbers to accurately reflect their own true costs.

a/ *See table 6, page 24*
b/ *See appendix tables A, B, and C (pages 57–61) for details of depreciation calculation*
c/ *Includes mulching plants in display beds*
d/ *Includes expendable sign materials*
e/ *Includes liability insurance*

at 3% but, in early years, it should be much higher to draw attention to the new business. Neither garden center was expected to have accounts receivable. However, bank credit cards were assumed for each.

As a percentage of sales, garden center A, after achieving its $1,000,000 in annual sales, was projected to have a profit of nearly $30,920, or 3.1%. Garden center B had $16,943 in operating profit on $350,000 in sales, or 4.8%.

For the above calculations, depreciation was derived using the straight-line method, depreciating the same amount each year (see the appendix tables B and C, pages 58–61). Tax regulations generally allow for a more rapid recovery of outlays for depreciable assets. Therefore, profits can vary considerably, depending upon the method used to derive the depreciation expenses in a given year.

Based on the percentage of sales, garden center B has a higher cost in salaries but less in insurance, depreciation, utilities, and repairs and maintenance. Also, because garden center B carried a smaller proportion of its sales in the relatively low markup hard goods, its gross profits expressed as a percentage were higher.

No attempt was made to project monthly income or cash flow statements, because seasonal sales vary widely among regions. However, Horticultural Research Institute's latest survey data were used to estimate the distribution of monthly sales (table 9) (HRI 1998).

Balance Sheets

Pro forma balance sheets were developed for both garden centers at the end of the third year (tables 10 and 11). There were at least two reasons for selecting a time period beyond the initial year. First, the year should represent a time period in which some depreciation has occurred. Second, for purposes of calculating returns on equity, a sufficient passage of time was needed for the garden center to fully develop its sales potential.

The balance sheets contained in tables 10 and 11 were based on the assumption of total ownership of the assets except for outstanding accounts payable. This situation is referred to as a 100% equity situation. However, very few start-up businesses are fully financed by the owner, so the effect of leveraging (borrowing a certain percentage of the initial start-up investment) would need to be analyzed. Garden center A represented a 3.2% return on equity (ROE) at 100% ownership, while garden center B had a return of 4.8% (table 12). Neither of these ROEs would be considered outstanding, because entering this type of business is considered to be a risky venture.

Managers of existing or prospective garden centers should be able to use the procedure outlined by adapting the material in tables 2–3 and 5–11 to conduct similar analyses for their respective situations. These model garden centers serve as an example to illustrate the evaluation process.

Table 9. Monthly sales distribution for garden centers A and B

MONTHS	TYPICAL PERCENTAGE OF ANNUAL SALES	MIDDLE RANGE
January	1.5	0.6–2.0
February	2.5	0.8–4.0
March	6.0	3.0–9.0
April	12.5	9.2–15.0
May	24.5	18.8–28.7
June	13.5	10.0–16.8
July	8.5	6.0–9.0
August	6.0	4.7–7.0
September	6.5	5.0–7.5
October	6.5	5.0–8.0
November	5.5	3.0–6.9
December	6.5	4.0–10.0

Source: Research Summary: HRI Operating Cost Study, *13th Edition, Horticultural Research Institute, Washington DC, 1998.*

Note: The typical percentages were adjusted to sum to 100.

Table 10. Pro forma balance sheet at end of third year of operation for garden center A with $1,000,000 in sales

ITEM	VALUE ($)
CURRENT ASSETS:	
Cash	10,000
Inventory [a]	105,757
TOTAL CURRENT ASSETS	**115,757**
FIXED ASSETS:	
Land [b] and improvements	667,128
Less depreciation	(65,136)
	601,992
Buildings	275,095
Less depreciation	(53,634)
	221,461
Equipment	88,180
Less depreciation	(31,377)
	56,803
TOTAL FIXED ASSETS	**880,256**
TOTAL ASSETS	**996,013**
CURRENT LIABILITIES:	
Accounts payable	35,000
TOTAL CURRENT	**35,000**
TOTAL LIABILITIES	**35,000**
EQUITY	**961,013**

Note: The numbers used for start-up costs and financial statements in this book are for illustration purposes only. They are not intended to reflect accurate estimates of the costs associated with establishing and operating a garden center. Garden center operators should use the charts and tables as guidelines for entering their own numbers to accurately reflect their own true costs.

[a] *Estimated by the ratio: Turnover = Cost of goods ÷ Inventory*
[b] *No depreciation was charged on land.*

Table 11. Pro forma balance sheet at end of third year of operation for garden center B with $350,000 in sales

ITEM	VALUE ($)
CURRENT ASSETS:	
Cash	2,500
Inventory [a]	36,190
TOTAL CURRENT ASSETS	**38,690**
FIXED ASSETS:	
Land [b] and improvements	276,848
Less depreciation	(14,502)
	262,346
Buildings	54,885
Less depreciation	(10,797)
	44,088
Equipment	21,445
Less depreciation	(7,542)
	13,903
TOTAL FIXED ASSETS	**320,337**
TOTAL ASSETS	**359,027**
CURRENT LIABILITIES:	
Accounts payable	8,500
TOTAL CURRENT	**8,500**
TOTAL LIABILITIES	**8,500**
EQUITY	**350,527**

Note: The numbers used for start-up costs and financial statements in this book are for illustration purposes only. They are not intended to reflect accurate estimates of the costs associated with establishing and operating a garden center. Garden center operators should use the charts and tables as guidelines for entering their own numbers to accurately reflect their own true costs.

[a] *Estimated by the ratio: Turnover = Cost of goods ÷ Inventory*
[b] *No depreciation was charged on land.*

Table 12. Effect upon return on equity (ROE) of alternative equity position for selected garden centers after three years of operation

	GARDEN CENTER					
	A – Percent equity			B – Percent equity		
ITEM	100	75	50	100	75	50
Income ($)	30,920	11,700	-7,521	16,943	9,932	2,922
Equity ($)	961,013	720,760	480,506	350,527	262,895	175,264
ROE (%)	3.22	1.62	-1.56	4.83	3.78	1.67

Note: Equity based on original investment depreciated for three years. Income for the 75% and 50% equity positions reduced by 8% interest on the debt.

PART 2: Financial, Marketing, and Business Principles for Garden Center Operation

PERSONNEL

The most important asset of an organization is the human asset, and the best measuring device for the quality of an organization is the quality of the people. Organizations with top-quality people are more profitable because they have the most satisfied customers, the best company image, and the ability to weather economic slumps. Finding and keeping good employees is a key management task.

Labor is an important issue in the green industry. In fact, the labor situation was cited as the number one concern of surveyed nursery people. Labor accounts for 26% of sales on average for the entire green industry. The cost of labor is not just the salaries earned by employees. There are many additional hidden costs such as social security, unemployment insurance, workers' compensation, and fringe benefits. See figure 6 (page 33) for an overview of the true cost of labor.

From outward appearances, the most obvious way to reduce labor expenditures is to hire fewer employees. This is usually a mistake. A better idea is to increase efficiency by careful hiring, effective training, motivational policies, and intelligent scheduling, which will in turn create a quality work force that is the asset your company needs to be successful. Labor is the direct link between the customers and the products and/or services offered by the business. Products and services affect the magnitude of those sales through the image of the garden center, the quality of the merchandise, the skills and knowledge of the employees and management, and the ability to satisfy customers' objectives. Customers buy more than plants, hard goods, or services; they buy expected benefits and satisfaction. A popular misconception is that the garden center is a horticultural enterprise when, in fact, the retail garden center is a people-oriented business that must rely on customers, employees, and managers to be successful.

Hiring/Selection

Since the cost of hiring and training a new person is significant, you should carefully select your employees in order to avoid costly mistakes. Poor personnel management creates a high turnover rate, resulting in greater expenditures for recruitment, selection, and training. It also reduces productive management time, drives away business, and increases the number of dissatisfied customers.

Develop a planned set of steps for your hiring process:

1. Write job descriptions and position specifications.
2. Get a pool of candidates.
3. Prescreen candidates based on the position's basic requirements.
4. Develop a list of interview questions.
5. Interview.
6. Describe the company and give a timetable.
7. Check references.
8. Make a clear offer.

Job Descriptions and Position Specifications

Job descriptions characterize a job and include the duties and responsibilities of the job as well as reporting communications relationships (figure 4). Position specifications characterize a person and include the essential behavior characteristics necessary for the job (figure 5, page 30).

Figure 4. Personnel form: job description

POSITION: GREEN GOODS EMPLOYEE

A. Garden Center Objective

To render effective service through a well-managed, soundly financed proprietorship established to improve the environment and customer satisfaction.

B. Reporting Relationships

Reports to Plants and Beds Supervisor.

C. Personally Responsible for the Following Activities

1. Assists with housekeeping of aisles, beds, plants, and premises.
2. Assists in maintaining plants inventory.
3. Assists with minor maintenance of plants and equipment.
4. Assists and waits on customers in a prompt, courteous, efficient, and knowledgeable manner.
5. Helps with unloading of incoming green goods and dry goods.
6. Assists other employees in the performance of duties assigned to the green goods section.
7. Attends staff and educational meetings as directed by supervisor.
8. Returns tools, equipment, and vehicles to their designated place after using them in the performance of duties.
9. Performs other activities as directed by supervisor.
10. Promotes a positive work environment.

D. Coordination and Communication Relationships

1. To lend full assistance to patrons and other employees for the growth and economic progress of the garden center in such a way as to build desired garden center image and good customer and employee relations.
2. To promote good will and seek every opportunity to develop understanding and acceptance of the business's plans, programs, objectives, products, and services.

A position announcement should include: the job's title; the experience and education necessary to do the job; duties and responsibilities of the position; the position's place in the company hierarchy; paths for advancement; on-the-job training periods; and the position's stated purpose, such as "to monitor and control pests so plants can be produced efficiently and free from insects and disease." It may also include personality traits and characteristics considered desirable for the job. A position announcement that accurately describes the job will help potential employees determine whether they will be happy in the position.

Recruiting

The most frequently cited sources of new employees are employment agencies (specializing in this industry), high schools, trade schools, colleges, universities, classified ads, and current employees. College internships, vo-tech high school programs, trade shows, and trade publications offer potential sources of employees.

Consider some nontraditional sources of employees. Part-time employees offer several advantages. They allow quick expansion of the work force to meet peak season/holiday workloads,

Figure 5. Personnel form: position specifications

POSITION: PLANTS AND BEDS SUPERVISOR

Department: Green Goods

Position Objective: To obtain, secure, and maintain quality plants for retail.

A. Duties and Responsibilities
   1. Answer customer questions politely and intelligently.
   2. Establish plant maintenance regime to meet quality control standards.
   3. Meter chemicals and irrigate plant inventory as needed.
   4. Maintain inventory controls and levels.
   5. Maintain clean and orderly aisles and plant beds.
   6. Check accuracy and appropriateness of point-of-sales materials and price cards daily.
   7. Maintain all necessary sales and inventory records.
   8. Assist and direct other employees in maintaining quality plants for retail sales.
   9. Assist customers in checkout and loading when appropriate.
   10. Identify problems and make suggestions to supervisor.

B. Skill Requirements
   1. Must be people-oriented.
   2. Must have landscape plant knowledge.
   3. Must have a college degree in horticulture, or equivalent work experience.
   4. Must understand production and marketing policies and procedures.
   5. Must be knowledgeable of consumer and environmental horticulture programs.

but they rarely expect or receive benefits or overtime pay. Some employees with full-time jobs want to supplement their income with another part-time position. Other people who have caretaking responsibilities at home are not available for full-time employment but can meet a part-time schedule. Assign a manager the responsibility for scheduling part-time employees.

Disabled persons have been found to be more reliable and loyal, have less absenteeism, and remain in their positions longer than other types of employees. Also, there are tax benefits associated with hiring disabled employees.

Interviewing

A comprehensive interview enhances the company's image with the candidates and sets the tone for the rest of the work experience. When management spends time conducting thorough interviews, candidates understand the importance of personnel to the firm.

Prepare for the interview by developing a worksheet to record behavioral characteristics required for the job. Plan a set of questions designed to discover those characteristics. Look for absolute traits that are essential for the job. Consider behavioral traits that provide some insight into how the candidate will be motivated.

Look at the interpersonal skills to discover how each person will work with the rest of your team.

Selection

Use the completed worksheets and notes on each candidate to review potential applicants. Compare each applicant to a standard (the position specification) and not to one another. Discuss the candidates with at least one other member of the management staff. Avoid snap judgments, but don't ignore the "hunch" you feel about a potential candidate. Notify the chosen candidate and conduct an expectation interview to review salary and benefits and to get a commitment from the candidate.

Legal Issues

Job applicants can file charges of discrimination if they can show that the gathering of even seemingly innocent information indirectly discriminates against them on the basis of sex, age, race, religion, handicap, or national origin.

Training/Retaining

Training can be divided into two categories: orientation and ongoing training. Offer an orientation for all new employees. Management behavior during the first day on the job will set the tone for the new employee's experience. One half hour of management time can mean the difference between a positive, upbeat beginning and a confusing, overwhelming one. Some employers try to spend a little time each day of the first week with new employees to offer coaching, encouragement, and guidance.

Employees need sufficient knowledge about a company's history, organization, key personnel, policies and procedures, products and services, market, and company niche. They also need to learn the key technical skills and people/ communication skills required for the job.

Ongoing training should include both in-house and outside training. Regular training sessions can be used to communicate new product knowledge and teach technical and communication skills. Design product knowledge training sessions to focus on the benefits for the customer rather than a product's technical performance. Teach sales people to listen to the customer's needs and present products that will meet those needs. Finally, use technical product features to substantiate the benefit claims.

Distinguish between behaviors and responsibilities. Responsibility is the desired outcome. For example, an employee might be responsible for keeping a seasonal display well-stocked. The behavior necessary to complete that task might include checking on the arrival of new merchandise, planning and executing the seasonal display, monitoring the display throughout the sales day to refill sold merchandise, and changing seasonal displays every two weeks. This definition of behavior clearly defines how management wants the employee to perform certain tasks. Training should include a description of how employees are actually supposed to do things. Include a time frame and materials required in the descriptions.

Evaluation

Conduct regularly scheduled performance evaluations. Allow the employee to conduct a self-evaluation first. Then schedule a performance review. Outline the procedure you will follow. Work from the job description for each employee. Specific job descriptions allow the manager and employee to work from the same checklist. As a result, behaviors are performed correctly or incorrectly, and evaluation is no longer a matter of opinion. Focus on observable, measurable components of a job that contribute to the organization's overall productivity and performance. Quality, quantity, timeliness, and cost are the four variables that can be measured and used to evaluate job performance.

At the end of the performance evaluation, agree on goals for the future. Document the discussion in each employee's file.

Termination

The current legal climate has made it difficult to fire an employee at will. The number of wrongful-discharge cases is increasing all the time. Even though most cases are settled out of court, the settlement and legal fees can be costly. To avoid unnecessary litigation, develop an employee-termination policy. Conduct regular employee evaluations and maintain records of the reviews. It is easier to discharge an employee with several written evaluations that document inadequate performance.

When you have to terminate an employee, make the termination interview as nonthreatening as possible. Assign the direct supervisor of an employee to conduct the termination interview. Avoid anger and personal attack.

Insurance

Workers' compensation is a significant expense for each employee. Workers' compensation laws and regulations vary from state to state. Consider implementing a self-insurance program, in which you save a specified amount per employee each pay period to cover potential claims. Couple such a program with aggressive safety training to reduce on-the-job injuries. Create a climate that values safety.

Labor Cost Estimation

Two main issues affect labor efficiency. The first is individual efficiency or job performance, and the second is adjusting the supply of the various qualities of labor available to meet job requirements. Hire excellent people who are well-suited to the assigned jobs. Motivate employees with a combination of pay incentives and work environment adjustments. Train employees to help them reach their full potential. Schedule employees efficiently by thoroughly understanding the needs of the business. Use the most significant asset of your company, your employees, to create a profitable and successful garden center business.

The following labor cost estimation worksheet (figure 6) provides a means for making these important estimates for workers and managers. To better understand this process, consider the following example that is appropriate for a garden center business. Similar analyses were performed for each of the employees in the model or representative firms in this study in order to attain appropriate labor costs and to evaluate the employee-sales performance ratings cited later.

The following facts comprise the example and are shown in the appropriate sequence for completing the worksheet and for estimating the cost-to-employer and income-to-employee levels.

- John Greenup, a plants and beds supervisor, is paid a base wage of $6.75 per hour for a regular 40-hour week and time-and-a-half for overtime hours, which average 15 hours per week during the spring and fall portions of the year.
- Each Christmas, the garden center pays a small bonus to its full-time employees, usually 2.5% of their base salary.
- Social Security (FICA) is currently 7.65% of total cash wages, being equally contributed by the employer and the employee.
- Federal and state unemployment insurance is calculated at 0.8% and 2.5%, respectively, of the first $7,000 of wages.
- Workers' compensation is figured at $4.14 per $100 of total cash wages.
- Group life insurance is provided at a cost of $17.11 per $1,000 of base wages (rounded to the next highest $1,000), and group medical-dental insurance is provided at $78.50 per month per employee.

Figure 6. Labor cost estimation worksheet

Name *John Greenup* Date *xx/yy/zz*

Title *Plants and Beds Supervisor*

Cost Item	Cost to Employer	Income to Employee
Direct wage costs:		
1. Total regular hours: hrs/wk *40* x *52* #wks	= *2,080* hrs	
Overtime hours: hrs/wk *15* x *16* #wks	= *240* hrs	
2. Cash wages (*2,080* hrs x *6.75* $/hr)	= $ *14,040.00*	= $ *14,040.00*
3. Overtime wages (*240* hrs x *10.125* $/hr)	= $ *2,430.00*	= $ *2,430.00*
4. Cash bonuses ($ ______ or *2.5* %)	= $ *351.00*	= $ *351.00*
5. **Total adjusted cash wages** (total lines 2 through 4)	= $ *16,821.00*	= $ *16,821.00*
Mandatory wage costs:		
6. Social Security (*7.65* %)	= $ *1,286.81*	= $ *xx*
7. Federal unemployment insurance	= $ *56.00*	= $ *xx*
8. State unemployment insurance	= $ *175.00*	= $ *xx*
9. Workers' compensation	= $ *696.39*	= $ *xx*
10. Other ______	= $	= $
11. **Total value of mandatory costs** (total lines 6 through 10)	= $ *2,214.20*	= $
Value of fringe benefits:		
12. Insurance — life	= $ *256.65*	= $ *256.65*
health/dental	= $ *942.00*	= $ *942.00*
other ______	= $	= $
13. Retirement (firm's contribution)	= $ *673.92*	= $ *673.92*
14. Uniform (purchase/rental/cleaning)	= $ *250.00*	= $ *250.00*
15. Transportation ______ mi/day x ____ days x ______ $/mi	= $	= $
16. Educational expense	= $ *250.00*	= $ *250.00*
17. Other ______	= $	= $
18. Other ______	= $	= $
19. **Total value of fringe benefits** (total lines 12 through 18)	= $ *2,372.57*	=$ *2,372.57*
20. **Total labor costs** (total lines 5, 11, 19)	= $ *21,407.77*	=$ *19,193.57*
21. Hours paid but not worked *Holidays *48* hrs; Vacation *80* hrs; Sick leave *96* hrs	= *224* hrs total*	= *224* hrs total*
22. **Total hours on the job** (line 1 *2,320* – line 21 *224*)	= *2,096* hrs	= *2,096* hrs
23. **Total costs per hour on the job** (line 20 divided by line 22)	= $ *10.21*	= $ *9.16*

- The business contributes 4.8% of base pay into a retirement plan.
- Aprons and jackets, with the name of the firm shown in large letters, are provided and laundered at a cost of $250 per employee per year.
- Up to $250 per year is provided for educational expenses.
- John Greenup receives six paid holidays and two weeks of paid vacation and is allowed to take an average of one day per month for sick leave each year.

Not all the items on the worksheet are applicable to every situation, but they are included to call attention to them and to avoid overlooking any direct or indirect costs. Note also that some items are costs to the employer but are not income to the employee.

The value of fringe benefits represents both the cost to the employer and the value or income to the employee. All the fringe benefits increase the employer's cost per productive man-hour and the employee's total remuneration package. These are the true figures (line 23) that both management and employee should use in evaluating their respective employment alternatives.

Thus, in the example described, $9.16 per hour, rather than the $6.75 wage rate, represents the appropriate labor cost figure for John Greenup to use when evaluating other employment opportunities. Estimates of this kind should be made for all employees to ensure that the proper labor cost numbers are used when estimating particular job or activity costs.

Allocation of Labor Costs for Garden Centers A and B

For garden center A, with annual gross sales of $1 million, the budgeted labor or personnel costs are $180,000 with an additional $50,000 for the manager/operator. The budgeted labor expenses for the smaller garden center B, with annual gross sales of $350,000, total $65,000 with an additional $30,000 for the manager/operator. An itemization of the functional employee types included in the respective budgets follows (table 13). Wage rates and labor expenses were calculated using competitive wage rates as supplied by the Department of Labor for 1991.

Table 13. Allocation of labor costs for garden centers A and B

GARDEN CENTER A	EMPLOYEE CATEGORY	GARDEN CENTER B
1 full-time @ $50,000	Manager/Operator	1 full-time @ $30,000
1 full-time @ $35,000	Plant Technician/ Cost of Goods Sold Manager	
1 full-time @ $25,000	Equipment Handler/Maintenance	
8 seasonal (13 wk) @ $3,350 each	Customer Assistance	5 seasonal (13 wk) @ $3,350 each
10 seasonal (13 wk) @ $2,620 each	Check-out Clerks	2 seasonal (9 mo) @ $16,625 each
2 full-time @ $20,000 each	Kiosk Information/ Assistant Plant Technician	
1 full-time @ $25,000	Accountant/Bookkeeper	1 half-time @ $15,000
2 temporary (6 wk) @ $1,000 each	Christmas Seasonal	

GARDEN CENTER CUSTOMERS

Managers set the tone for employees' focus on the customer. When employees have this customer focus, they are better able to identify and meet customer needs. How do employees get a better understanding of customers and their needs? It begins with a general understanding of garden center clientele. It then proceeds to asking questions on a formal or informal basis to learn more about one garden center's specific clientele.

The Average Customer

The average garden center customer is likely female and between the ages of 25 and 55. In one study of approximately 1,600 garden center customers, the average shopper was 48 years old with a median household income of $45,000. The average household had two to three residents. Many (65%) were college graduates and most (80%) were married. Of the married respondents, approximately half had children. Overall, about 75% of the shoppers were female.

Age Influences

People tend to have friends who are a similar age with similar interests. Researchers who study consumers noticed that people of a similar age also have similar spending and saving patterns. These spending and saving patterns are influenced by the shared life experience people of the same age have. Since they are at a similar age, they also have similar needs and buy similar products to meet those needs.

Several general trends affect consumer spending, and the aging of Americans is one of those trends. Susan Mitchell identified five age groups in *American Generations*: GI or WWII Generation, Swing Generation, Baby Boomers, Generation Xers, and The Millennium Generation.

GI or WWII Generation

GI or WWII Generation individuals were born before 1933. They account for 14% of the population, a small group with limited resources. Tom Brokaw wrote about this age subculture in *The Greatest Generation*. They are great markets for health care products, but they are not great gardening customers nor are they likely to be in the future.

Swing Generation

Swing Generation individuals were born between 1934 and 1945. They are also a small group, accounting for only 14% of the American population, caught between two powerful forces. They are good gardening customers but will decline in importance. They are in retirement and may have smaller residences with limited gardening spaces. They are good markets for container gardening (especially vegetables and herbs), but not big markets for services, as they have frugal values on spending and saving.

Baby Boomers

Baby Boomers comprise the largest percentage of Americans today (30%) and were born between 1946 and 1964. They are in their first or second career, raising families, and building large homes. Their aging has fueled the economic growth of the country, and they are prime gardening customers. While they're working full-time, they are time-constrained and are a good target for services. These customers are the heart of the garden center customer base, because they own homes and are actively engaged in landscaping and gardening. However, garden centers need to be aware of how the aging of Boomers—and their eventual retirement—will affect garden center spending.

Generation Xers

Generation Xers were born between 1965 and 1976 and comprise 17% of the population. The relative small size of this group has contributed to the labor shortage. They are entering their careers and buying first homes. They are quite well-educated but not as materialistic as their Boomer predecessors. They are focused on experiences.

Marketing gardening to them demands a different approach. Since they are focused on experience, they are looking for either active or passive ways plants can enhance their homes and lives. Approach them differently than you would Baby Boomers.

The Millennium Generation

The Millennium Generation includes people born between 1977 and 1994. They represent the next big economic boom, as children of Baby Boomers. They are in school now (many of them) but have tremendous economic buying power already. They also have busy schedules and will likely keep them that way. They are the most culturally diverse generation and have the opportunity to integrate traditions and components of more than one culture into their lifestyles (good gardening opportunities). Recruit them as the next generation of gardeners by getting them actively involved in gardening, and nurture their love of plants early.

Groups of Gardeners

Gardeners differ in their motivation for gardening. An understanding of these motivations helps you target specific products to meet individual needs. *Organic Gardening* magazine researchers identified four segments, or groups, of American gardeners (published in *American Demographics*, April 1983) that show differences by gardening motivation. These segments are still useful for understanding garden center customers today.

Sales-Based Groups

Dabblers accounted for 61% of gardeners but only 50% of sales. They spend only a few hours in the garden each week and may prefer doing something else. They are not the core market segment who shops in the traditional retail garden center but may become one if they develop a passion for gardening.

Cultivators accounted for 18% of gardeners and 17% of sales. These gardeners are mainly interested in vegetable gardening. Approach them in the garden center with ideas and products that meet their desire to get a harvest from the land. Decorative items or color-coordinated flowers won't appeal to them as much as new vegetable cultivars or ways to increase yield.

Decorators accounted for another 18% of gardeners but 29% of sales. They color coordinate flower color with home decor. They bring living space outdoors in decks and patios. They spend more time and money in the garden. Focus products and ideas to them that beautify and enhance their homes and outdoor living spaces. Use color-coordinated plants with matching furniture cushions to catch their eye.

Masters accounted for 3% of gardeners and only 4% of sales. Use them as "opinion leaders" by giving them new plants to try in their own gardens. They have lots of friends who ask them gardening questions. Recruit them as marketing allies, and get feedback from them frequently. Give them new plants to try, and ask them to tell you about that plant's performance. They are great candidates to try new products. When they are successful, they will tell their friends. You will want them to tell YOU about plant failures so no other gardeners experience the same problem.

The American Nursery and Landscape Association recently completed a study of gardeners. Their *2000 Grapevine Survey* findings confirm the *Organic Gardening* magazine categories. Using similar but different terminology, ANLA found that gardening motivation and enjoyment shaped customer groups. (To order a copy of the *2000 Grapevine Survey,* contact the American Nursery and Landscape Association, 1250 I Street NW, Suite 500, Washington, DC 20005; phone 202-789-5980; WWW.ANLA.ORG)

Time-Based Groups

Maintainers accounted for 7% of gardeners who spent about five hours weekly in the garden.

Seeking a passive experience, they want to enjoy, not work in, the garden. They will spend fewer dollars than hobbyists and dedicated investors (see below). Show them how to save time and market services to them, keeping in mind their passive desires. Price will be high on their list, so perhaps give a menu of choices so they can select the services in which they are most interested.

Passive Investors accounted for 14% of gardeners who spent an average of eight hours weekly in the garden. This group is also seeking a passive experience and is mainly interested in keeping up appearances. They may spend more money than maintainers and are another great target market for services, given their passive nature. However, they are very aware of appearances and may be more likely to spend dollars on services.

Novices accounted for another 17% of gardeners who spent nearly nine hours weekly in the garden. They are just learning and usually less loyal customers but show promise and potential. They may evolve to become another type of gardener. Provide active and passive experiences for these newcomers to gardening. Identify their needs and limitations to more concisely target products and services to them, being aware that they will develop interests and change to resemble another segment.

Chores accounted for 19% of gardeners who spent about nine hours weekly in the garden. They would rather spend time on other pursuits and, like the maintainers, are more interested in enjoying their garden than working in it. They are not likely markets for many gardening products and services, other than those that save time or make their lives easier.

Hobbyists accounted for 21% of gardeners who spent nearly 13 hours weekly in the garden. They garden for enjoyment and are involved in multiple projects. They spend more and seek an active gardening experience, much like the masters and the decorators. Garden centers should provide hobbyists with in-store hands-on opportunities, as they are a prime market for many products and services.

Dedicated Investors accounted for 23% of gardeners who spent about nine hours weekly in the garden. Gardening is a lifestyle for them, and they enjoy active roles and passive roles in gardening. They comprise the heart of the garden center market and are ripe targets for educational and escapist experiences.

CUSTOMER SERVICE

Customer service is the provision of courtesy and kindness extended in the process of delivering a product. It is critical to garnering repeat business and building customer loyalty. Companies that understand the lifetime value of a customer place significant emphasis on excellent customer service. It is much easier to retain current customers than prospect for new customers (Barton 1999). Yet somehow, many businesses fail to keep their customers. When asked why customers stopped purchasing from a store, the reason provided by the greatest number of respondents (68%) was that they were treated poorly by a salesperson or employee (St. John and Fish 1998). Whiteley (1991) reported that customers are five times more likely to switch vendors due to perceived service problems than to price or product quality concerns. Customers in an Oklahoma survey cited unfriendly help and lack of prompt service as the most common complaints related to service (Henderson and Schnelle 1991). Service quality delivered by employees is a key to business success.

Plant quality and selection consistently rank as the most important reasons for selecting a retail outlet (Khatamian and Stevens 1994; Makus et al. 1992). However, access to a trained professional sales staff often was selected as the third most important reason for retail outlet selection. A focus group study (Safley and Wohlgenant 1995) indicated that a majority of potential customers expect independent garden centers to have better quality plant material than mass merchandisers, because garden center personnel are better trained to care for the plants. Product sourcing has enabled many retailers to obtain the high product quality desired by most customers. This leaves service quality as an important differentiation opportunity.

In a 2000 customer preference survey (Behe and Barton 2000), respondents ranked plant quality as the most important dimension (30%) contributing to a garden center's quality. Willingness to help customers and provide prompt service as well as the knowledge and courtesy of personnel and their ability to convey trust and confidence were both about half as important to respondents (15%). This survey supports the conclusion of many other surveys that plant quality (32%)—in this case defined as plant health—is more important to customers than plant price (22%) (Henderson and Schnelle 1991; St. John and Fish 1998).

When customers' perceptions are compared to their expectations at a garden center, the difference represents a service or product quality gap. In a series of questions assessing plant and product quality, respondents reported that the largest gap and therefore weakest performance was in meeting customer expectations for clearly marking the price of plants. The survey also assessed service quality and found that there is room for improvement in all areas of service quality (Behe and Barton 2000).

Garden centers should focus on stocking and maintaining only the healthiest plants. Respondents placed the highest priority on plant health and condition, and a significant gap currently occurs in the ability of participating garden centers to meet customer expectations. Another way to address plant health is to offer a guarantee in case the plant does not survive. Garden centers could better meet customer expectations by providing plant guarantees. Plant assortment and variety was also fairly important to respondents, but garden centers are doing a better job of meeting customer expectations in this category. An additional area for improvement is plant labeling, especially with the price. For inexperienced customers or those who spend little, this factor is important.

Many customers (72%) purchase plant material and supplies from more than one firm (Padgett et al. 1965). Research has found that customers who frequently shop for plants generally spend more money at one particular outlet, consequently acquiring a greater number of plants from that outlet (Behe and Barton 2000). In a 2000 study, more frequent purchasers had greater store loyalty to the outlet at which they were surveyed. The ability of employees to convey knowledge and trust was more important to consumers who spent more at the garden center. Garden centers are doing a good job of providing service to customers who spend significant amounts of money or make frequent purchases yearly in their establishments. However, consumers who spend less money yearly do not have lower expectations for service, so one strategy to enhance customer relations would be to provide quality service to all customers, not just the frequent buyers with whom the sales people are familiar. This strategy might turn the less frequent buyer in to a more frequent buyer.

MERCHANDISING

Marketing is a process by which an individual identifies market opportunities, selects a target market, then develops and implements a plan for business success. Merchandising, the second step in the marketing process, is defined as "all the business activities that increase profitable sales."

This process involves both increasing the size of the customer base and increasing profitable sales per customer. Merchandising should promote sales at a price that secures a reasonable return on investment. Differentiation, the process by which a product or business is perceived as being different and better, is one mechanism used to accomplish the goals of merchandising.

Merchandising is a very broad strategy that incorporates many diverse programs, each with its own specific objective. The approach emphasizes a profit focus, not just sales. Coordination among programs is essential. If a customer sees a product advertised and goes to the store with serious buying intentions, but then leaves without making a purchase, a portion of the program has failed. When one program fails, the entire merchandising effort is jeopardized.

Eight factors that are generally recognized as constituting the merchandising package include business image, layout and displays, product mix, promotion, advertising, labels, logo, and pricing strategy. Four of these factors are considered essential for operating a nursery business profitably—layout and displays, promotion, advertising, and pricing.

Layout and Displays

Layout is one of the major factors that contributes to the success of any garden center. A garden center should be designed to maximize sales and minimize the cost of selling. Careful consideration of how to make the garden center more convenient for both customers and employees will result in increased sales and reduced expenses.

Powell (1990) illustrated the importance of good layout and display as a means of attracting customers. Results of a survey of 2,000 retail garden center customers indicated that they first learned about a garden center because they (1) passed it on the road or (2) heard about it from a friend or neighbor (word-of-mouth) (figure 7). An attractive, highly visible, and convenient garden center provides a better source of new and repeat

Figure 7. How customers first learned about a garden center

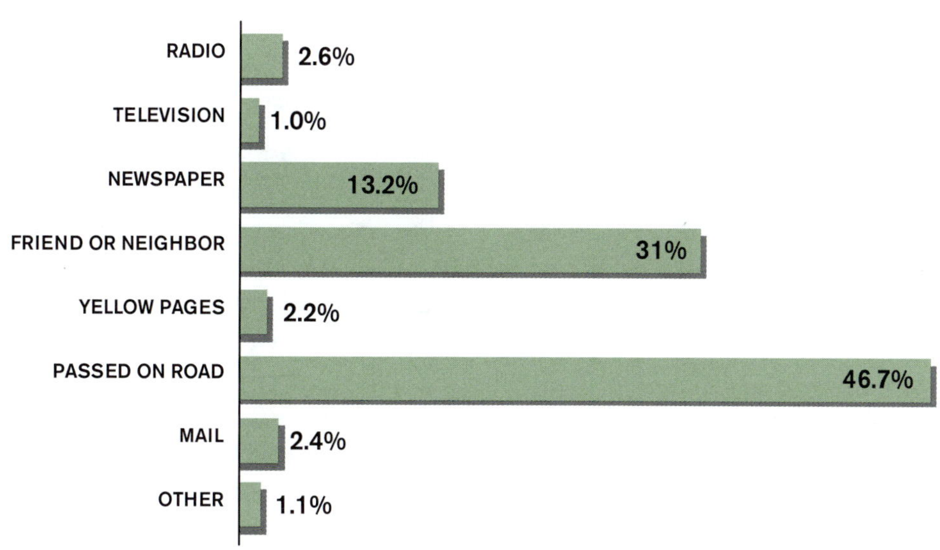

customers than expensive marketing efforts through various print and broadcast media. A garden center should entice people to stop, and the entire garden center must fulfill the customer's expectations to ensure repeat visits and word-of-mouth publicity.

For customers, merchandise should be displayed so it is attractive, inviting, easy to locate, and accessible. For employees, the layout must facilitate rapid restocking and offer a clear view of the entire sales area to help identify customers who may need assistance and discourage shoplifting.

Attracting Customers

The garden center preferably should be located on a well-traveled road with a safe and convenient entrance and exit. The sign is the first visual impression made on potential customers and should project an appropriate image. A simple sign with large letters reads more easily than a cluttered sign with too much information (Barton 1986).

Attractive landscaping that uses colorful plants around the sign and along the road frontage draws attention to the garden center. Attractive and well-maintained display gardens can build a garden center's image and attract the attention of passing motorists. Poorly maintained display gardens are a negative advertisement for the plants and project an unsatisfactory business image. Temporary displays of balled and burlapped (B&B) and containerized plant material make alterations and removal of deteriorated plant material easier, but increase watering requirements. Irrigation systems and mulching reduce the amount of additional care required.

Parking

The parking lot should be easily accessible, clearly defined, and large enough to accommodate all cars, even on the busiest spring weekends. Ideally, the parking lot should be paved and lined to indicate parking spots to eliminate wasted space. Crushed stone is an acceptable alternative to asphalt, but is difficult to negotiate in high heels—a problem since 75% of all garden center customers are female. Angled parking reduces the area required between rows for maneuvering.

Convenient Shopping

The garden center should promote convenience with merchandise that is both visible and accessible. Customers entering the front door should be able to quickly determine the general location of major departments within the store and the direction to the greenhouse and nursery yard (Weatherly 1977). This flow can be accomplished with the use of attractive displays and effective signage. Aisles at least four feet wide, parallel to the entrance, and double glass doors to the greenhouse and nursery yard will improve visibility for both customers and employees.

Merchandise should be located between knee and eye level. Display depth for small items should be limited to an arm's length (about two feet).

Carts will make shopping more convenient and encourage additional purchases. Smooth floor surfaces and large or balloon-type tires will increase cart maneuverability.

Encouraging Sales

The goal of store layout is to direct customers through as much of the store as possible. The more products customers see, the more they are likely to buy. Stocking popular or high-turnover items in the far corners or in out-of-the-way yet highly visible locations encourages shopper circulation. Low-turnover merchandise, companion products, and high-priced items should be stocked on the pathways between popular items or between the popular products and the checkout counter. Good traffic flow reduces the number of dead corners and ineffective selling locations (Weatherly 1977).

Layouts can be placed into three general categories—a grid system, free-form layout, or boutique layout. A grid layout is easy to design but boring and may not encourage browsing. A free-form layout, while less space efficient, encourages customers to browse and creates a luxury image. The longer customers stay in the store, the more they are likely to buy. In a boutique layout, products are linked together into functional displays. For example, a display of bulb planters, bone meal, gloves, pots, and other related items located around the bulb boxes can encourage tie-in sales.

Point-of-purchase displays at strategic locations in the store will increase add-on and impulse sales. Signs can be incorporated into displays to provide general product and product-use information.

Signs are the most important means of communication with the customer. Signs are used to direct traffic flow, identify plants and other products, and provide additional information. Photographs showing plants in full bloom will promote sales when plants are not in their prime. Signs can help reduce labor costs and provide information customers need when sales people are too busy to assist everyone. Many customers will still need or want personal assistance with special problems or concerns, but signs can be used to answer routine questions and make silent suggestions.

Checkout and Loading

To the extent possible, checkout areas should be located between the parking lot and the merchandise. When checkouts are located near exits, customers are exposed to all products and have the opportunity to make selections before they pay. Customers are unlikely to return to the checkout once a purchase has been made, even if they see a desirable item. Checkout counters are prime areas for relatively inexpensive impulse items.

Cash registers located on islands allow two lines to be served at the same time. One checkout can be located inside with a window to the outside. This checkout area services both inside and outside, eliminating the need to bring heavy shrubs into the sales room. A temporary checkout can be set up outdoors to increase efficiency during peak sales times. All checkouts require provisions for electrical, computer, and telephone cables.

Bulky items such as bagged mulch and peat moss should be located near the parking lot and inside the fenced area. Efficient loading reduces labor requirements and costs.

Restocking

Rapid restocking is essential to prevent lost sales due to empty displays. Displays that appear empty discourage sales by giving the impression that only poor-quality merchandise remains. Displays arranged to facilitate rapid restocking reduce labor costs and release sales people to assist customers and sell merchandise.

Space Utilization

Displays should be consolidated as products are sold to create the appearance of good product selection and to utilize empty space for new displays. A small, dense display of high-quality plant material is more desirable than a large display with empty spaces. Low-quality plant material or hard goods in damaged packages take up valuable space and detract from the overall display appearance.

Adaptability

Space requirements change from season to season and from year to year. Departments must be expanded and consolidated with alterations made as quickly and easily as possible. A flexible layout and display system allows garden centers to meet the changing needs of their customers. A garden center located near new housing developments may have a large market for trees and shrubs at first, then experience declining sales for these products and increased demand for annuals, fertilizer, mulch, and other maintenance products as the market matures. A garden center must stay in touch with consumer wants and needs to know when the product mix should be altered.

Promotion

Promotion refers to communication efforts designed to influence potential and existing clients. These communications can be grouped into two broad categories: personal selling and nonpersonal selling. Personal selling involves direct interaction with potential customers, while nonpersonal selling includes all demand-creation activities other than personal selling. Nonpersonal strategies should be used to attract customers to the store, and the personal approach is helpful once the prospect has arrived. Three promotional efforts (awareness of the product, comprehension of what is offered, and conviction that the product is worth buying) constitute the sales process.

Although sales-promotion tools (coupons, contests, premiums, and so forth) are highly diverse, they have three distinctive characteristics: (1) communication—they gain attention and usually provide information that will lead the consumer to the product; (2) incentive—they incorporate some concession, inducement, or contribution that gives value to the consumer; and (3) invitation—they include a distinct invitation to engage in the transaction now. If used properly, sales-promotion tools can create a stronger and quicker response to the product offered. Although they can be effective at boosting sagging sales, sales-promotion benefits are usually short-term. In the long run, the ability to consistently provide quality products and service will determine sales and profitability.

Promotional tools are limited only by one's imagination. Some examples include:

- Contests, games, and sweepstakes
- Premiums and gifts
- Trade-in allowances for plants or garden tools
- Fairs and trade shows where products are exhibited
- Tie-in merchandise like T-shirts and bumper stickers
- Open house with a seasonal theme (Halloween, Christmas, Easter)
- Plant shows or auctions with prizes

The goal of these promotional activities is to draw people into the store; however, they don't all have the same effects. Promotion can be used to increase the customer base, increase sales per customer, or enhance the business image. The type of strategy used will be influenced by the specific objective of the business.

If the objective is to increase the customer base (attract new clients), programs like plant shows, contests, and open houses where refreshments are served and small prizes are awarded are useful. Programs focused toward children have an influence on a parent's decision of where to shop.

To increase sales per customer, concentrate on rewarding regular customers. Since these are the least expensive customers to attract, show appreciation by offering discounts on selected items, gift certificates after a certain amount of purchases, or free potting service for "special" customers. Attaining customer loyalty should be an ongoing effort, because loyal customers will buy again, talk favorably to others about the business, pay less attention to competitors, and purchase new products that the business later adds to its product line. Regular customers are a precious commodity and should be treated as such.

If the goal is to enhance the business image, plant shows and plant competitions are useful where the garden center's best products are displayed. Holding an open house for school children is also an excellent way to generate positive publicity. Publicity is appealing because of its high credibility. News stories seem more authentic and credible than advertisements, because the message gets to the buyers as news rather than as sales-directed communication. Many businesses tend to underuse product publicity or use it as an afterthought. Yet a well-thought-out publicity program coordinated with other promotional elements can be extremely effective.

Advertising

Advertising is one of the four principal tools that businesses use to direct persuasive communication to target buyers. It consists of nonpersonal or one-way forms of communication conducted through paid media under clear sponsorship. In the commercial sector, the percentage of sales spent on advertising varies considerably, from a low of 1.6 for the automobile industry to a moderate amount for soft drinks (6.5), candy (6.6), and soap (7.5) to very high for perfumes (11.5) and record albums (22.5) (Kotler 1988). A range from 3 to 5% of sales was presented for horticultural retail operations in the Horticultural Research Institute's *Retail Operating Cost Study* (1998).

In developing an advertising program, it is important to have a clear understanding of the target market and factors that stimulate and motivate those in it. With this information, positive product attributes can be matched to the preferences of potential consumers. The sale becomes easier when a close match is made. With knowledge of market and consumer desires, the retailer can begin to address five major decisions known as the five Ms of advertising (Kotler 1988):

- Mission: What are the advertising objectives?
- Money: How much can be spent?
- Message: What message should be sent?
- Media: What media should be used?
- Measurement: How should the results be evaluated?

Setting Advertising Objectives

Many different communication and sales objectives can be assigned to advertising. An advertising goal is a specific communication task and achievement level to be accomplished with a specific audience in mind over a specific period of time. Examples of advertising objectives include increasing foliage plant sales to household customers by 10% within one year or increasing the sale of tie-in products by 20%. Advertising objectives fall into three categories: to inform, to persuade, and to remind.

Informative advertising can be used early in the business life cycle, when a sizable shift in business emphasis is made (for example, when adding a major service component), or simply to communicate to customers that new and interesting plant varieties are available. This objective is to build primary demand.

Persuasive advertising is important in a highly competitive market to differentiate a business from others by building selective demand. An advertising theme should focus on a business's comparative advantage. A garden center may offer exceptional selection, quality, service, dependability, or shopping convenience; a unique garden environment for generating "ideas;" or fun and safe play areas for the children. With persuasive advertising, one business points out the difference between what they have to offer and the competition. Although this approach is commonly used (for toothpaste, automobiles, fast foods, and soaps, for example) it can be interpreted negatively or cause competitors to behave similarly.

Reminder advertising is used to keep customers thinking about an established business. Expensive, four-color Coca-Cola advertisements in magazines are used not to inform or persuade but remind people to purchase Coca-Cola. Reinforcement advertising is used to let people know they have made the right choice in coming to a particular garden center.

Determining the Advertising Budget

Each business must spend enough money on advertising to attain its advertising goals. This figure is difficult to determine. Spending too little will achieve insignificant results, while overspending suggests some of that money could have been put to better use. Four common methods for determining advertising budgets are employed by many firms today (Kotler 1988). These are summarized below.

Affordable Method. Many companies set the advertising budget based on what they think they can afford. This method ignores the role of advertising as an investment and its immediate impact on sales volume. It can lead to an uncertain annual advertising budget, making long-range planning very difficult.

Percentage-of-Sales Method. Many businesses set advertising expenditures as a specified percentage of sales (either current or expected) or of the sale price. While it has the advantage of simplicity, the percentage-of-sales method uses a roundabout way of thinking. Sales are seen as the cause of the advertising rather than the result. Budgets are set by the availability of funds rather than by the opportunities available in the market. The dependence of the advertising budget on year-to-year sales fluctuations also interferes with long-range planning. Finally, the method does not provide a logical basis for choosing the percentage figure, except by using what has been done in the past or what competitors are doing. This conservative approach allows little flexibility for developing the type of advertising budget a garden center may really need.

Competitive-Parity Method. This method assumes that by spending the same percentage of sales as its competitors, a business will maintain market share. Such an approach raises questions about whether competitors are spending the right amount; how competitors arrive at their figures; and whether a business can differentiate itself from competitors when it is copying them.

Objective-and-Task Method. A more sound and aggressive approach is to develop advertising budgets by defining specific objectives. After determining what goals and objectives are to be accomplished within a given time frame, a business should provide the necessary budget to get the job done. For example, if the objective is to market the garden center to residents of a new housing development, determine the costs required to promote your garden center in that part of town.

Choosing a Message

It is not necessarily the size of an advertising budget that determines effectiveness but rather the quality of message transferred. An advertisement can improve sales only after gaining the attention of the target market. Creative strategies are indispensable to successful advertising.

The easiest way to discover what is important to the target market is to interact with customers. Finding out what customers like most and least about a garden center will provide important clues to a creative strategy. A good advertisement should focus on one central selling proposition without trying to provide too much information. The message should promote the garden center's desirable and interesting qualities, distinguish itself from other advertisements, and present itself in a manner that the customer finds believable.

The effectiveness of the message depends not only on what is said but also on how it is said. The choice of headlines, words, letter size, and color all affect how the message will be received. A copy strategy statement describing the objective, content, and tone should be developed for each ad. The headline or major theme is key, because few people take time to read the body of the text.

Selecting the Media

Media selection involves determining the maximum number of targeted prospects that can be reached within the constraints of the advertising budget (Kotler 1988). This will largely be determined by the reach (the number of different people exposed to a particular media schedule at least once during the specified time), frequency (the number of times within the advertising period that the average person or household is exposed to the message), and impact (the quality of the exposure when it reaches client prospects) of the media. Reach is most important if a business is new to an area, while frequency is more important if a garden center is trying to project a particular image. The garden center's targeted market should be considered when selecting media, since different media target different segments of the population.

Due to the costs involved, most garden centers have a limited selection of media. Typically, garden centers use newspapers, trade journal magazines, local magazines, direct mail, and maybe radio. A few large garden centers in small markets can utilize local television.

Evaluating Advertising Results

The final evaluation of an advertising program is whether the campaign fulfilled the advertising objective. Measurement is a difficult task. Garden centers can use coupons; questionnaires; traffic monitoring before and after a campaign; requests for additional information from a newspaper or radio ad; or a comparison of sales figures. An evaluation of traffic counts and sales could provide an indication of immediate impact; however, the cumulative impact of advertising is more difficult to ascertain. No single measure will yield a conclusive pronouncement on the effectiveness of an ad campaign.

Pricing

The objective of any business is to generate an acceptable return on investment (ROI). Simply stated, a garden center should price products to cover costs and generate an acceptable net return. Unfortunately, the task of identifying and allocating all fixed and variable costs is not as simple as it may seem. Cost is not the only factor to consider when setting prices. A successful pricing strategy includes an analysis of personal and business objectives, the competition, the market, and consumer price limitations.

Prices may be determined based on cost, intuition, imitation, or any combination of the three. Cost-based prices are computed by adding desired markup to the cost of goods. Intuition prices are based on what the manager thinks the customers are willing to pay. Imitation-based prices are set below, at, or above those of competitors. Setting prices in relation to the competition's prices is dangerous, because overhead and variable costs are different for every garden center. One garden center may make a profit at a certain price, while another garden center loses money due to higher costs. A successful pricing strategy should incorporate an analysis and implementation of all three pricing methods.

Pricing is a process that results in profit or losses. Costs, customers, and competition may change, and prices must be adjusted as these changes occur. The first step is to gain a thorough knowledge of the total cost of each product or service offered. The second step is to determine whether a market exists for that product or service at that price.

A three-way balance among selling prices, sales volume, and expenses is required. Low prices may generate a high sales volume but may not produce enough income to cover expenses. High prices may not generate enough volume to cover expenses. The overall objective is to produce the largest total profit, not the largest profit per item or largest sales volume.

Understanding Costs

Total costs include variable, fixed, and overhead costs. Variable costs are those that vary directly with the level of sales, such as materials, labor, and transportation. Fixed costs remain constant regardless of the level of sales, such as mortgage payments, property taxes, and insurance. Overhead may consist of both fixed and variable costs. For example, the cost of a bookkeeper paid an hourly wage will increase as the workload increases with higher sales. The cost of the bookkeeper is variable but not directly associated with any single product, so this variable cost should be included in overhead.

Overhead costs are usually allocated as a percentage of sales or a percentage of space required for a product. When overhead is allocated as a percentage of space, the percentage must be adjusted to reflect the length of time the space is occupied by each product. Annuals may take up 10% of the total display area, but since they occupy 10% of retail space for six months, only 5% of overhead should be added to their cost. Until a historical pattern is established, allocation as a percentage of sales or space is no better than an estimate. However, with this estimate, all costs are accounted for, even if they are somewhat incorrectly allocated.

Break-Even Analysis

A breakdown of costs into fixed, variable, and overhead categories facilitates calculation of the best selling price using break-even analysis. Break-even analysis provides a method for determining the minimum level of sales and the selling price required to break even. It also allows owners to evaluate the impact of various changes in costs on break-even sales.

The minimum level of sales can be used to assess the profitability of each product line before any money is spent. The break-even point (BEP) is calculated from the profit equation, where profit is set at zero.

$$\text{Profit} = 0 = [(P - DC) \times Q] - OH$$

P = selling price per unit; Q = quantity sold;
DC = direct cost per unit (variable cost);
OH = overhead

By rearranging the equation, one can solve for the quantity (Q) needed to reach the BEP:

$$Q = \frac{OH}{(P - DC)}$$

In the following example, the manager of a garden center expects to sell 200 fruit trees in the coming year at $15 each. It costs $13 per tree to buy and prepare the trees for sale. The portion of overhead costs allocated to these trees is $300.

How many trees must be sold to break even?

$$Q = \frac{OH}{(P - DC)} = \frac{\$300}{(\$15 - \$13)} = \frac{\$300}{\$2} = 150 \text{ trees}$$

What is the profit if the expected 200 trees are sold?

$$\begin{aligned} \text{Profit} &= [(P - DC) \times Q] - OH \\ &= [(\$15 - \$13) \times 200] - \$300 \\ &= \$400 - \$300 \\ &= \$100 \end{aligned}$$

The sale of 200 trees would net a $100 profit. The analysis also shows that sales can fall 25% below the forecast level of sales before the business loses money.

By rearranging the break-even formula, it is possible to determine a break-even selling price (P) that is consistent with the expected overhead cost, direct cost per unit, and sales volume. In the previous example,

$$\begin{aligned} P &= \frac{OH}{Q} + DC \\ &= \frac{\$300}{200} + \$13 \\ &= \$1.50 + \$13 \\ &= \$14.50 \text{ per tree} \end{aligned}$$

Break-even analysis can be used to make adjustments as costs, sales volume, and market conditions change.

Understanding the Market

Costs and break-even calculations must be tempered with knowledge of the garden center market. An understanding of the customers, their needs, the competition, and how the competition might react will help each garden center determine the cost the market will bear. Once determined, a price can be changed to reflect changes in cost, demand, or competition, but prices that change too frequently may lead to confusion or distrust on the part of the consumer.

Prices must be justified by value (or perceived value) to the customer. New cultivars, plants available in limited quantities, novelties, or items that are uncommon or new all command higher prices. Promotional or "traffic-generating" items may justify lower prices.

Research has shown that unlike many other retail industries where products are perceived to be identical, price is not the most important factor in governing a customer's choice of where to shop for plant material. Factors more important to customers include plant selection, plant quality, and service (Powell 1990) (figure 8).

Margin versus Markup

Margin and markup are terms that are often misunderstood. Markup is the percentage of cost added to the cost to determine the selling price. Margin is the percentage of the selling price that is gross profit. Fifty percent added to the cost does not yield a 50% margin. Fifty percent markup yields only a 33⅓% margin.

Alternative Pricing Strategies

Psychological Price Barriers. Price barriers are a series of check points consumers use to determine the relative value of a product (Marciel 1989). Major price barriers exist at \$1, \$5, \$10, \$15, \$20, and so forth (table 14, page 48), and are common to all consumers. Minor barriers exist at \$1.50, \$2.00, \$3.00, \$7.00, and so forth (table 14), and their importance varies depending on the need for the product, desire for the product, and amount of discretionary income. The objective is to set prices just below a price barrier. Table 15 on page 49 provides an easy reference for determining prices using psychological price barriers.

If attaining the desired profit margin causes a price to fall above a price barrier, it is best to price the

Figure 8. Why customers shop at a particular garden center

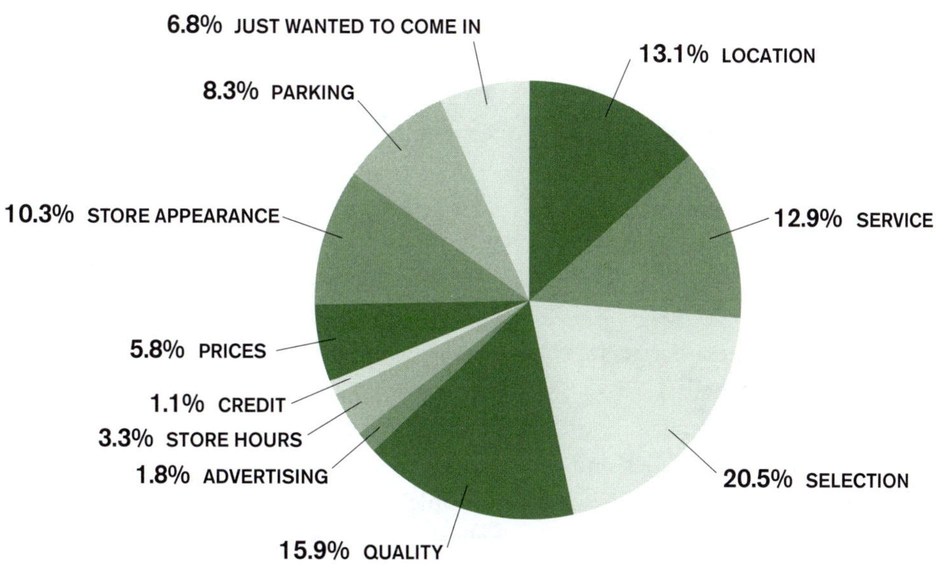

Table 14. Price barriers in the garden center industry

MAJOR PRICE BARRIERS	MINOR GREEN GOOD BARRIERS	SUGGESTED PLANT PRICES	MINOR HARD GOOD BARRIERS	SUGGESTED HARD GOOD PRICES
1.00	–	0.99	0.50	0.49
–	1.50	1.49	1.50	1.49
–	2.00	1.99	2.00	1.99
–	–		2.50	2.49
–	3.00	2.99	3.00	2.99
–	–		4.00	3.99
5.00	–	4.99	–	4.99
–	–		6.00	5.99
–	7.00	6.99	7.00	6.99
–	8.00	7.99	8.00	7.99
–	–		9.00	8.99
10.00	–	9.99	–	9.99
–	13.00	12.99	13.00	12.99
15.00	–	14.99	–	14.99
–	17.00	16.99	17.00	16.99
–	18.00	17.99	18.00	17.99
20.00	–	19.99	–	19.99
–	23.00	22.99	23.00	22.99
25.00	–	24.99	–	24.99
30.00	–	29.99	–	29.99
40.00	–	39.99	–	39.99
50.00	–	49.99	–	49.99
75.00	–	69.99	–	69.99
100.00	–	99.99	–	99.99
150.00	–	149.99	–	149.99
200.00	–	199.99	–	199.99

Note: Once a customer jumps a price barrier, resistance drops dramatically until the next barrier is approached. The greater the price, the greater the distance to the next price barrier.

product just below the next highest barrier. The customer will not perceive that increase in price, and the garden center will receive a greater total profit since the same number of units will be sold, each at a higher profit.

The importance and usefulness of these barriers vary with the type of product and whether substitutes are readily available. The distance between price barriers for chemicals, mulches, and other hard goods is smaller than for plants, because differences in quality are not as evident and price competition among retailers is greater.

Variable Pricing. Hidden costs such as perishability and special handling requirements are often overlooked in pricing, resulting in a lower than expected profit margin (Marciel 1989). When plants require special care or handling, are very perishable, or are subject to greater than usual breakage losses, the base cost can be adjusted by adding allowances for hidden costs. The following example illustrates how to establish the "real" cost before pricing an unusual, difficult-to-maintain

Table 15. Suggested retail prices for green goods

COST ($) FROM	TO	RETAIL PRICE ($)[a]	MAXIMUM GROSS PROFIT MARGIN (GPM) (%)
0.00	0.44	0.99	–
0.45	0.58	1.29[b]	65
0.59	0.63	1.49[b]	70
0.64	0.76	1.79[b]	64
0.77	0.90	1.99	61
0.91	1.12	2.49[b]	63
1.13	1.35	2.99	62
1.36	1.80	3.99[b]	66
1.81	2.25	4.99	64
2.26	3.14	6.99	68
3.15	3.60	7.99	61
3.61	4.50	9.99	64
4.51	5.85	12.99	65
5.86	6.75	14.99	61
6.76	7.65	16.99	60
7.66	8.09	17.99	57
8.10	9.00	19.99	59
9.01	10.35	22.99	61
10.36	11.25	24.99	58
11.26	13.50	29.99	62
13.51	18.00	39.99	66
18.01	22.50	49.99	64
22.51	31.50	69.99	68
31.51	45.00	99.99	68
45.01	58.50	129.99[b]	65
58.51	67.50	149.99	61
67.51	76.50	169.99[b]	60
76.51	90.00	199.99	62

[a] *Based on a minimum gross profit margin of 55%*
[b] *Suggested prices between barriers for a competitive market*

plant such as hibiscus and a common, easily maintained plant such as dwarf mugho pine that were purchased for $11.00.

	Hibiscus	Pine
Purchase price	$11.00	$11.00
Add: Perishability (10%)	1.10	0
Add: Special care/handling	0.50	0
Actual cost	$12.60	$11.00
Sale price @ 55% gross profit margin	$28.00	$24.45
Price barrier adjustment	$29.99	$24.99

Quality Differentiation. A pricing strategy that merits consideration is allowing customers to buy the quality they can afford. Any shipment of plants contains plants of varying quality. If all the plants from one shipment are priced the same, the good quality will sell first and a selection of poor-quality plants that look overpriced remains. Instead, a median price for each plant from that shipment can be calculated and high-quality plants priced higher, medium-quality plants priced at the median price, and low-quality plants priced lower than the median. Customers then have the option of buying the price and quality combination they desire.

Price Skimming. A "skimming" strategy is when prices are set high initially, then gradually reduced. Customers who want the product will pay the higher price, leading to higher short-term profits. This strategy is most successful with a new or unusual product that is without direct competition. If the price is set too high, it can be lowered. Lowering prices is much easier than raising prices. Many people associate quality with price, and they may be more willing to pay higher prices because of perceived enhanced value. This phenomenon is usually only a short-term strategy, because having high prices and profits encourages the development of substitutes and is subject to increased competition.

Penetration Pricing. For "penetration," prices are set deliberately low in an attempt to gain a large share of the market. Once the market share has been gained, prices are gradually raised to maintain an adequate profit margin. This strategy discourages competition, because other stores are not able to sell the product at a profit. However, other stores may attempt to compete by lowering their prices, resulting in lower profits for everyone. If customers subsequently resist price increases, the retailer is prevented from achieving an acceptable return.

Volume Discounts. Volume discounts are often referred to as "multiple unit" pricing. The objective is to encourage customers to purchase greater numbers by offering discounts for larger quantities. Customers must be clearly informed of the cost saving in order for the volume discounts to be effective.

Discounting. Garden center operators are usually too quick to lower prices. There are times, such as the end of the season, when discounting may be appropriate; but, discounting has a dramatic effect on profit. Twice as many plants (wholesale cost $6.00) must be sold at a selling price of $8.00 in order to make the same profit as those sold at $10.00. The objective of dramatic discounting is to reduce inventory. The "buy one, get one free" approach accomplishes that objective more quickly than offering 50% off.

Proper pricing is a procedure that must be developed for a particular market. Prices must be evaluated regularly and adjusted based on costs and market changes.

DIVERSIFICATION

From a manager's point of view, the simpler a business and the more defined its purpose, the easier it is to understand. When resources are channeled through fewer production and marketing activities, management can more easily supervise, direct, and monitor the business.

A simple business is less likely to have problems. With a complex business, more activities or processes can go wrong, and when they do, it is more difficult to find and isolate the problem. Because they have more activities to manage, complex businesses have more bureaucratic layers to coordinate. Each additional product or service line requires inputs, tasks, and trained personnel.

Planning assumes a more vital and urgent function in a highly diversified firm. Decisions are more complex, and management must interpret the business through abstract forms, quantitative data, complex lines of communication, and reports rather than through firsthand experience. For instance, a manager responsible for ordering large quantities and varieties of perennials will place a more accurate order if he or she maintains close ties with customers as opposed to relying solely on a computer scan sheet.

Given the evidence against diversification, one must consider conditions or circumstances under which diversification may be warranted, or even desirable. These conditions can be categorized into internal and external pressures for diversification (Drucker 1985).

Internal Pressures

One important reason to diversify is to prevent or minimize boredom from repeating the same tasks. Change results in exposure to new ideas and concepts. These new ideas nurture and stimulate interests that improve the business and keep its employees happy.

A second incentive to diversify is to reduce the risks associated with maintaining the same product or service line year after year. A complete line of standard clay pots will not continue to keep market share when attractive ceramic and plastic pots become available elsewhere. Stocking specialty products for too long can be risky.

A third reason to diversify is to convert an internal cost center into a revenue-generating outlet. This approach can result in firms integrating forward or backward into adjacent economic stages. Businesses using costly inputs may find it advantageous to develop them in-house and, if profitable, sell these inputs as new product lines. A garden center may begin growing plants that are unavailable in sufficient quantity and quality from its current suppliers or may develop a landscape company to install the plants it sells. However, effective diversification should be consistent with the mission and market strategy of a business. The business must maintain the characteristics that distinguish it in a positive way from the competition.

External Pressures

Diversification may be warranted when the market is limited to the point that it restricts business growth. When there is no opportunity for expansion and the business is too small to remain viable, it may be necessary to diversify into related product lines. For example, retail gasoline stations moved away from a narrow sales base of petroleum products and services into a broader line of food, beverages, and a variety of reading materials. In the late 1970s and early 1980s, these businesses were driven to identify and implement innovative ways to add profitability to shrinking petroleum margins.

A garden center that specializes in landscape-size plants may need to expand its product lines to include items such as ready-to-use potted plants when the surrounding community matures and new landscaping is no longer prevalent.

Business diversification can also result from market expansion. In the 1950s through the 1970s, market demand within the fast-food industry was fairly constant. Food varieties were limited, and the target market was confined largely to teenagers. Two significant social developments—women entering the labor force and Americans' desire for healthy and nutritious foods—caused the fast-food market to mushroom and redefine its operations. The garden center industry has many opportunities to create new products and services based on current demand for convenient and environmentally sound products.

Technology is a third external pressure pushing businesses toward diversification. An innovation for one product serving one market can evolve into multiple products serving several markets. For instance, tissue culture is a technology that has dramatically affected the foliage plant industry. Months or years of painstaking propagation has been replaced by rapid multiplication of uniform plants with greater selection than previously possible.

A low-risk and commonly employed method of expanding the garden center's business is simply to increase "bread and butter" products to existing markets. However, when this approach is no longer profitable, more diversified and riskier strategies may be required. Three possible strategies are (1) market diversity—sell existing products to new markets; (2) product or service diversity—sell new or improved products to existing markets; and

(3) product-market mix—sell new products to new markets. The greatest risk is assumed with this last strategy, because both product and market environments are new. Regardless of the approach ultimately chosen, it is important to have product or service expertise on hand prior to embarking on a diversification effort. Many factors should be considered, such as the requirements for minimum investment, selection, display space, storage space, services, hours of operation, management time, trained staff, and compatibility with current business. While cut flowers are another horticulture product, the full-service florist business has many service and staff requirements that are not required for a garden center.

When dealing with a new product or service area, it is important to invest sufficiently to achieve what is called a "critical mass." In other words, there must be sufficient variety, selection, and quality so the new enterprise is capable of attracting customers and is a viable profit center unto itself.

Ultimately, success with diversification depends on the business's ability to maintain a common core of unity among the different organizational entities. Decisionmakers must know how much diversity the business can sustain without jeopardizing what it does best. Also, management must be careful not to extend its efforts to an area or extent that it is inefficient.

FINANCIAL ANALYSIS

Although ratio analysis is the most common form of financial analysis, two other performance-measuring tools are (1) checking the garden center's financial progress over time (time-series analysis) and (2) comparing the business's performance against other garden centers (cross-sectional analysis). For example purposes, garden center A will be used for comparison in the financial analysis.

Comparisons over Time

The information contained in table 7 (page 25) represents one year's data to allow for an historical comparison of the income statements. Once data are available for three years (or longer), the progress of the firm can be more effectively evaluated. A common tendency is to limit the analysis to the dollar change in product items over time. This practice provides little information on the business's real performance. A more useful analysis should include both changes in profit levels and percentages of sales across time periods.

All expense items should be examined carefully, especially the larger components. A garden center manager may find that some expense items actually decline as the sales volume increases, simply because total expenditures change little with respect to sales. If the same physical facilities are used over time, depreciation and/or rent would decrease, as a percentage of sales, as the volume of sales increases. Similarly, purchasing expenses decline as a percentage of sales as trade sources become established. Savings could be realized through fewer trips to markets and may decline by placing larger orders.

Assuming the owner-manager has not been including his or her income from the business in the salary statement, profits will represent earnings for the value of labor and management plus return on investment. Ideally, larger profits should reflect growth in the value of management and in the value of investment. An unchanging profit level indicates the owner is not receiving enough for management and investment, even though in the latter case equity may be increasing.

Observing the balance sheet over several years provides a basis for checking a business's progress toward financial stability (table 10, page 27). Indicators are the value of assets, amount owed (liabilities), and the owner's equity. Converting the data to percentages expresses the values as a ratio of assets. One of the more frequently used indicators is the percentage of the business that is owned relative to outside claims against assets: debt to equity. This measure reflects the solvency of the firm. A measure of liquidity or the ability to meet short-term obligations is the current ratio: current assets to current liabilities.

Inflation and changing real estate values should also be considered when analyzing historical trends in the balance sheets. Values of assets and liabilities typically are entered at the current values at the time of the transaction. After a few years of rapidly rising real estate values, the balance sheet may not realistically reflect asset market values. For some purposes, valuing assets at current market value is a useful exercise. Two such events in which current market values are needed would be for estate planning and when maximum equity is needed for additional financing.

Interfirm Comparisons

Another useful form of analysis is to compare the financial position of the business with other businesses that are of similar type and volume. Collection of financial information for garden centers has been inconsistent; therefore, suitable information for comparative purposes may not be readily available.

However, options do exist. One of the most applicable benchmarking publications is the *Retail Operating Cost Study* published by Garden Centers of America (ISBN 1-890148-01-6, WWW.ANLA.ORG). Also, for a fee, firms such as Dun and Bradstreet can supply garden center financial ratios. Other possibilities include state Cooperative Extension systems, ornamental horticulture departments of land-grant universities, state trade associations, and information from various trade magazines.

Some progressive garden center managers work out arrangements with businesses of similar type and size to compare financial data and other information. Possibilities for trading information are limited only by the imagination of those involved. For instance, some businesses cooperate in state surveys (such as the Cooperative Extension system), where data are used to calculate industry averages. In this way, confidentiality is guaranteed for individual businesses.

Prior to making comparisons, it is crucial that comparable accounting procedures have been applied to the businesses being compared. Two areas in which the greatest differences are likely to occur are the handling of the owner-manager's salary and the charge for the use of the physical facilities. In some cases, nearly all the facilities may be rented, while in other cases, everything is owned. The proper procedure is to adjust the accounting system to a common method.

In dealing with the owner-manager's salary, the most logical approach is to add the salary as an expense if it is not already included. Regardless of how much was withdrawn, the amount used should reflect the value of the contribution made to the business. If other family members worked without compensation, the owner-manager's salary should also realistically reflect this.

In order to handle the facility cost problem, those businesses not renting the land and buildings should make a charge reflecting rent on comparable properties. This approach requires an estimate of the current market value of the facilities. Interest paid on mortgages and other long-term obligations should then be excluded from expenses but deducted from operating income to generate net income. Interest on short-term loans is included.

Adjustments are also needed for the balance sheet when they are not developed on a similar basis. The adjustment in this case involves removing the garden center from the real estate business, in the event the land and buildings are owned.

RATIO ANALYSIS

Financial ratios provide a shorthand means of communicating information about a business. Although ratios can provide valuable insights into a business, they do have limitations. As ratios become available over time for a garden center, and as ratios are made available for similar businesses, their value improves.

Financial ratios are classified by their sources of data. First, balance sheet ratios indicate how the business stood at a given point in time. Second, income statement ratios indicate the results of operating the business for a period of time. A third type of ratio is composed of items from both the balance sheet and the income statement.

There is no universal agreement among the experts on which ratios to use in a financial analysis. The nature of the operation and goals and objectives of management serve as major guides to the importance of different ratios. However, ratios are not a substitute for management; instead, they are but one tool to help managers make more informed financial decisions. The ratios that follow are among the most widely used.

Balance Sheet Ratios

The more popular balance sheet ratios indicate how the business can meet current (liquidity) and future (solvency) obligations. The first has to do with working capital—the difference between current assets and current liabilities. The issue raised is how the business would settle up if current debts had to be paid suddenly. The ratio between these items is referred to as the current ratio. Using data from table 10 (page 27), the calculation is:

$$\text{Current ratio} = \frac{\text{Current assets}}{\text{Current liabilities}} = \frac{\$115{,}757}{\$35{,}000} = 3.3$$

Some might argue that inventories have little immediate value and should be omitted. This modification, referred to as the acid-test ratio, is:

$$\text{Acid-test ratio} = \frac{\text{Current assets} - \text{Inventory}}{\text{Current liabilities}} = \frac{\$115{,}757 - \$105{,}757}{\$35{,}000} = 0.3$$

Many consider a current ratio of 2:1 as a conservative minimum level. Others would argue that some inventories cannot be converted readily to cash to settle immediate debts, justifying the need for the acid-test ratio. If inventories are highly marketable, a lower ratio may be acceptable. Perishable and poorly marketable inventories may justify having a higher standard. If the items remaining in current assets after removing inventory are readily marketable, a 1:1 acid-test ratio is acceptable.

Since most businesses have accounts receivable—a third major item of current assets—an acceptable acid-test ratio is more likely to be achieved. The assumption of no accounts receivable, in this model, made the comparison directly between cash on hand and accounts payable. When seasonal inventory is being increased, accounts payable may exceed cash on hand. A high liquidity measure may reflect the firm's ability to take advantage of opportunities such as special purchases and quantity discounts.

For long-term financial questions, solvency ratios are useful. Debt holders are more interested in what proportion of the business is owned. These measures indicate how the lender would fare in the event of business failure, because those having external claims on assets (creditors) would have a preferential claim to equity holders.

These ratios can be expressed in several ways. But the more straightforward method uses a 50% equity situation:

$$\text{Solvency} = \frac{\text{Equity}}{\text{Total assets}} = \frac{\$480{,}506}{\$996{,}013} = 0.48 \text{ or } 48\%$$

The 48% represents ownership of the total assets.

Another measure of solvency is the relationship between fixed assets and equity:

$$\text{Solvency} = \frac{\text{Fixed assets}}{\text{Equity}} = \frac{\$880{,}256}{\$480{,}506} = 1.83 \text{ or } 183\%$$

This ratio implies that the owner's capital is tied up in fixed investments such as real estate and equipment.

Income Statement Ratios

Actually, the percentages as a proportion of sales shown in table 9 (page 26) are ratios from the income statements. Expressing items from the income statement as a percentage of sales is a popular method for analyzing a business's performance over time and in relationship to others.

The most popular of these ratios measures net profit:

$$\text{Net profit} = \frac{\text{Net profits}}{\text{Sales}} = \frac{\$30{,}920}{\$1{,}000{,}000} = 0.031 \text{ or } 3.1\%$$

Another frequently used ratio is the gross profit or gross margin, as a percentage of sales:

$$\text{Gross profit} = \frac{\text{Sales} - \text{Cost of goods}}{\text{Sales}} = \frac{\$1{,}000{,}000 - \$496{,}000}{\$1{,}000{,}000} = 0.504 \text{ or } 50.4\%$$

Similarly, other items are expressed as a percentage of sales. Two other commonly used items for garden centers are salary and advertisement costs:

$$\text{Salary cost} = \frac{\text{Salary expenses}}{\text{Sales}} = \frac{\$276{,}000}{\$1{,}000{,}000} = 0.276 \text{ or } 27.6\%$$

$$\text{Advertising cost} = \frac{\text{Advertising expenses}}{\text{Sales}} = \frac{\$30{,}000}{\$1{,}000{,}000} = 0.03 \text{ or } 3.0\%$$

Acceptable income statement ratios are often used as if they must be met in order to be successful. However, the underlying circumstances must be known before interpreting these ratios. For example, suppose one garden center produces its bedding plants, purchases foliage plants for growing out, and plants its hanging baskets. Another garden center purchases all of its plant materials ready for sale. The first business will likely show a relatively high gross profit but also a high salary cost. The second garden center will tend toward a lower gross profit and lower salary cost.

Often recommendations are made on advertising expenditures in relation to sales. Generally, these recommendations are for advertising to consist of at least 2–3% of sales. No consideration is given to the cost of advertising among different locations. With widely varying advertising rates, the same advertising expenditures may result in considerably different public exposure.

Ratios Composed of Items from Balance Sheets and Income Statements

Some of the more useful ratios require data from both the income statement and the balance sheet. Perhaps the best measure of profits or returns on investment is the ratio of profits to equity, also known as net worth:

$$\text{Profit on equity} = \frac{\text{Profit}}{\text{Equity}} = \frac{\$30{,}920}{\$961{,}013} = 0.032 \text{ or } 3.2\%$$

If profits do not include a charge for the owner-manager and other unpaid family labor (as was done for the data in table 7, page 25), the above ratio should be adjusted:

$$\text{Profit on equity} = \frac{\text{Profit} + \text{Charge for owner's labor}}{\text{Equity}}$$

The 3.2% represents the ratio of earnings on the owner's equity investment in the business and can be compared to alternative rates of returns that might be earned. Thus, the measure appears to be the perfect measure of profits; however, if asset market values are substantially different from the accounting values on the balance statement, a more meaningful ratio can be obtained after adjusting equity to current market values.

Another ratio used for comparative purposes is average inventory turnover. The calculation may be made from several income statement and balance sheet items, but cost of goods and an estimate of the average inventory over the period are as good as any.

$$\text{Inventory turnover} = \frac{\text{Cost of goods}}{\text{Average inventory}} = \frac{\$496{,}000}{\$105{,}757} = 4.69 \text{ times}$$

This ratio is for comparative purposes and is not intended to measure physical turnover.

Another method of checking the efficiency of working capital involves the average collection period on credit sales. Several methods may be used to make the estimate. Since the garden center was assumed not to provide credit, this ratio is not demonstrated. One method estimates average daily credit sales and divides this number into the average amount of accounts receivable during the year.

$$\text{Average daily credit sales} = \frac{\text{Credit sales for the year}}{365}$$

$$\text{Average collection period} = \frac{\text{Average accounts receivable}}{\text{Daily credit sales}}$$

The figure represents the number of days that credit sales are tied up before being received. This figure should be compared with the garden center's policy on credit to determine whether the average collection period is good or bad.

In summary, a business's progress can be measured in many ways. But three of the more meaningful methods are in terms of (1) comparing the garden center's records over time, (2) comparing its performance with other similar sizes and types of garden centers, and (3) computation of financial ratios for analysis.

Appendix Table A. Office equipment for garden center A with annual sales of $1,000,000, 1991

ITEM	QUANTITY	COST PER UNIT	COST
Desk	2	$367	$734
Chair [a/]	2	190	380
Filing cabinet	4	89	356
Metal bookshelf	2	125	250
Flat work table	2	185	370
Drafting table	1	140	140
Stool	1	40	40
Large metal cabinet	1	200	200
Desktop copier	1	895	895
Chair [b/]	4	75	300
Chair [c/]	12	50	600
Laminator	1	1,200	1,200
Time clock	1	335	335
PC computer	1	3,500	3,500
Laser printer	1	1,700	1,700
Software [d/]	1	1,000	1,000
TOTAL			**$12,000**

Note: The numbers used for start-up costs and financial statements in this book are for illustration purposes only. They are not intended to reflect accurate estimates of the costs associated with establishing and operating a garden center. Garden center operators should use the charts and tables as guidelines for entering their own numbers to accurately reflect their own true costs.

[a/] *Sidearm, swivel with rollers*
[b/] *Side chair*
[c/] *Stacking chair*
[d/] *Allowance*

Appendix Table B. Initial cost and annual depreciation for garden center A with sales of $1,000,000, 1991

ITEM	INITIAL COST	USEFUL LIFE (YEARS)	ANNUAL DEPRECIATION
LAND			
Unimproved land	$400,000	–	–
Improvements	100,000	20	$5,000
Parking lot	51,925	10	5,192
Parking bumpers	1,333	10	133
Security fence	22,948	10	2,295
Security chains	450	10	45
Sign	5,000	10	500
Security lights	12,000	10	1,200
Loading area	5,130	10	513
Service road	37,383	10	3,738
Display beds	9,209	10	921
Irrigation	8,000	10	800
Landscaping	13,750	10	1,375
TOTAL LAND AND IMPROVEMENTS	**$667,128**		**$21,712**
BUILDINGS			
Sales building	$192,000	20	$9,600
Greenhouse and work area	42,000	10	4,200
Overwintering greenhouses	8,000	10	800
Lath shade	6,510	10	651
Pole barn	8,500	10	850
Bulk bins and apron	3,985	10	398
Interior display shelves	5,000	10	500
Cashier counters	2,000	10	200
Gazebo	5,000	10	500
Benches	1,800	10	180
Information center	300	10	30
TOTAL BUILDINGS	**$275,095**		**$17,909**
TOTAL LAND AND BUILDINGS	**$942,223**		**$39,621**
EQUIPMENT			
Office equipment	$12,000	5	$2,400
Pickup truck	15,000	10	1,500
Truck	20,000	10	2,000
Skid loader	25,000	10	2,500
Water cooler	370	10	37
Fire extinguishes	560	10	56
Cash registers	2,000	10	200
Credit card scanners	1,840	10	184
Scales	50	10	5
Customer wagons	4,050	10	405
Utility nursery carts	1,000	10	100
Tree dollies	400	10	40

(Continued on next page)

Appendix Table B. Initial cost and annual depreciation for garden center A with sales of $1,000,000, 1991
(continued from previous page)

ITEM	INITIAL COST	USEFUL LIFE (YEARS)	ANNUAL DEPRECIATION
EQUIPMENT			
Hand trucks	500	10	50
Wheelbarrows	400	5	80
Sprayers (backpack)	200	5	40
Sprayer (hand pump)	40	5	8
Proportioner	200	10	20
Drop spreader	45	5	9
Lawn mower	250	5	50
Hand tools	800	10	80
Water hoses	375	5	75
Watering wands	100	5	20
Signs	3,000	5	600
TOTAL EQUIPMENT	**$88,180**		**$10,459**
GRAND TOTAL	**$1,030,403**		**$50,080**

Note: The numbers used for start-up costs and financial statements in this book are for illustration purposes only. They are not intended to reflect accurate estimates of the costs associated with establishing and operating a garden center. Garden center operators should use the charts and tables as guidelines for entering their own numbers to accurately reflect their own true costs.

Appendix Table C. Initial cost and annual depreciation for garden center B with sales of $350,000, 1991

ITEM	INITIAL COST	USEFUL LIFE (YEARS)	ANNUAL DEPRECIATION
LAND			
Unimproved land	$200,000	–	–
Improvements	50,000	20	$2,500
Parking lot	4,135	10	414
Parking bumpers	363	10	36
Security chain	150	10	15
Display beds	6,715	10	672
Roadside sign	1,000	10	100
Landscaping	3,469	10	347
Lights	4,000	10	400
Irrigation	3,500	10	350
TOTAL LAND AND IMPROVEMENTS	**$273,332**		**$4,834**
BUILDINGS			
Sales building	$37,800	20	$1,890
Storage building	500	10	50
Greenhouse	8,000	10	800
Enclosed walkway	300	10	30
Work area	500	10	50
Overwintering houses	4,000	10	400
Lath	1,240	10	124
Benches	1,050	10	105
Interior display shelves	1,000	10	100
Cashier counters	500	10	50
TOTAL BUILDINGS	**$54,890**		**$3,599**
TOTAL LAND AND BUILDINGS	$328,222		$8,433
EQUIPMENT			
Pickup truck	$15,000	10	$1,500
Office furniture	1,050	5	210
Fire extinguisher	140	10	14
Scales	50	10	5
Water cooler	370	10	37
Cash register	500	10	50
Credit card scanners	460	10	46
Hand tools	300	5	60
Wheelbarrows	200	5	40
Drop spreader	45	5	9
Sprayers	200	5	40
Tree dolly	200	10	20
Lawn mower	250	5	50
Two-wheel hand truck	250	10	25
Utility nursery cart	200	10	20
Customer wagon	1,080	10	108
Proportioner	200	5	40

(Continued on next page)

Appendix Table C. Initial cost and annual depreciation for garden center B with sales of $350,000, 1991
(continued from previous page)

ITEM	INITIAL COST	USEFUL LIFE (YEARS)	ANNUAL DEPRECIATION
EQUIPMENT			
Water hose	150	5	30
Watering wand	50	5	10
Signs	1,000	5	200
TOTAL EQUIPMENT	**$21,695**		**$2,514**
GRAND TOTAL	**$349,917**		**$10,947**

Note: The numbers used for start-up costs and financial statements in this book are for illustration purposes only. They are not intended to reflect accurate estimates of the costs associated with establishing and operating a garden center. Garden center operators should use the charts and tables as guidelines for entering their own numbers to accurately reflect their own true costs.

Literature Cited

American Appraisal Associates, Inc. 1991. *1991 Agricultural Building Cost Guide.* Milwaukee, WI: American Appraisal Associates, Inc.

Baldwin, Ian and John Stanley. 1982. *The Garden Centre Manual.* Portland, OR: Timber Press.

Barton, S. S. 1999. "Improving Customer Relations." *Garden Centers of America Newsletter* (April/May).

Barton, Susan S. 1990. *Garden Center Management: A Teaching Manual.* University of Delaware Cooperative Extension.

Barton, Susan S. 1986. *Garden Center Management: A Guide.* University of Delaware Cooperative Extension.

Behe, B. and S. Barton. 2000. "Consumer Perceptions of Product and Service Quality Attributes in Six U.S. States." *Journal of Environmental Horticulture* 18(2): 71–78.

Coyle, J., E. Bardi, and J. Langley, Jr. 1996. *The Management of Business Logistics.* Sixth Edition. St. Paul, MN: West Publishing Co.

Drucker, Peter R. 1985. *Management: Tasks, Responsibilities, Practices.* New York: Harper and Row, Publishers.

Feather, Frank. 1990. Produce Marketing Association Meeting, New Orleans, LA.

Gallup Leisure Activities Index. 1989. Princeton, NJ: Gallup Organization, Inc.

Guth, William. 1974. *Organizational Strategy: Analysis, Commitment, Implementation.* New York: Irwin Publishing Company.

Henderson, J. C. and M. A. Schnelle. 1991. *Oklahoma's Retail Nursery/Garden Center Industry: Marketing Practices and Sales Strategies.* Oklahoma Agricultural Experiment Station Bulletin B-798.

Hewitt, F. 2001. "After Supply Chains, Think Demand Pipelines." *Supply Chain Management Review* (May/June). Newton, MA: Cahners Supply Chain/OEM Group.

Johnson, Doyle C. 1998. "1998 Floriculture and Environmental Horticulture," *Outlook '98.* Washington, CD: United States Department of Agriculture, Economic Research Service.

Khatamian, H. and A. Stevens. 1994. "Consumer Marketing Preferences for Nursery Stock." *Journal of Environmental Horticulture* 12: 47–50.

Kinsey, J. 2000. "A Leaner, Faster Supply Chain: New Uses of Information Technology." *American Journal of Agricultural Economics* 82(5): 1123–1129.

Kotler, Phillip. 1988. *Marketing Management: Analysis, Planning, Implementation, and Control.* Sixth Edition. Englewood Cliffs, NJ: Prentice Hall.

Kurt Salmon Associates. 1993. *Efficient Consumer Response: Enhancing Consumer Value in the Grocery Industry.* Food Marketing Institute Report #9-526 (January). Kurt Salmon Associates: Washington, DC.

Lee and Whang. 2001. *Supply Chain Management Review* (March/April). Newton, MA: Cahners Supply Chain/OEM Group.

Makus, L. D., J. C. Foltz, J. F. Guenthner, and R. R. Tripepi. 1992. "Product and Service Attributes Related to Marketing Nursery Stock." *HortTechnology* 2: 483–487.

Marciel, Ron. 1989. Ohio Florists Association Bulletin No. 714. April 1989.

McGraw-Hill Information Systems Co. 1990. *Dodge Assemblies Cost Data*. Princeton, NJ: McGraw-Hill.

Mitchell, Susan. 1998. American Generations: Who The Are. How They Live. What They Think. Second Edition. Ithaca, NY: New Strategist Publications, Inc.

"Ornamental Horticulture Industry Is Blooming." 1988. *Agricultural Outlook* (July).

Padgett, J. H., Wilbur Mull, and T. L. Frazier. 1965. "Effect of Merchandising Practices by Retail Nurserymen on Consumer Buying." Georgia Agricultural Experiment Station Bulletin N.S. 140, pages 5–35.

Phillips, Travis D., Jr. 1990. Personal Communication. Starkville, MS: Phillips, Inc.

Porter, Michael. 1980. *Competitive Strategy: Techniques for Analyzing Industries and Competitors.* Free Press, A Division of Macmillan Publishing Co.

Powell, Russell. 1990. *Garden Center Customer Survey Report*. Penn State Cooperative Extension.

Principles, Practices, and Comparative Costs of Overwintering Container-Grown Landscape Plants. 1986. Southern Cooperative Series Bulletin 313. The Pennsylvania State University.

Research Summary. 1998. *HRI Operating Cost Study*. Thirteenth Edition. Washington, DC: Horticulture Research Institute.

Ross, D. F. 1999. *Competing Through Supply Chain Management*. Norwell, MA: Kluwer Academic Publishers.

R. S. Means Company, Inc. 1990. *Means Site Work Cost Data*. Kingston, RI: R. S. Means Company, Inc.

R. S. Means Company, Inc. 1990. *Means Building Construction Cost Data*. Kingston, RI: R. S. Means Company, Inc.

Safley, C. D. and M. K. Wohlgenant. 1995. "Factors Influencing Consumers' Selection of Garden Centers." *Journal of Agribusiness* 13(1): 33–50.

Schermerhorn, Richard W. 1978. *Economic Feasibility Analysis: What Is It and How Should It Be Done.* Misc. Publication 153 (February). University of Hawaii Cooperative Extension Service.

St. John, D. and L. Fish. 1998. "Creating Customer Loyalty." *American Nurseryman* (February 1, 1998) 64.

Stack Office Supplies. Doylestown, PA.

U.S. Bureau of the Census. *Census of Business-Retail Trade.*

U.S. Bureau of the Census. *Statistical Abstract of the U.S.*

U.S. Department of Agriculture. 1990. *Economic Indicators of the Farm Sector: State Financial Summary, 1989.* ECIFS 9-2. Washington, DC: Economic Research Service.

Weatherly, Neal Jr. 1977. *Home and Garden Supply Merchandiser* (December).

Wertheim, E. 1991. *Program Organization and Preparation for Schematic Planning* (August). San Francisco, CA: Wertheim, van der Ploeg, and Klemeyer Assoc.

Wertheim, E. 1989. Personal Communication. San Francisco, CA: Wertheim, van der Ploeg, and Klemeyer Assoc.

Whitley, R. C. 1991. *The Customer-Driven Company*. Reading, MA: Addison-Wesley.

Other Books from NRAES

The books described below are available from NRAES. To order, contact NRAES for current prices and shipping and handling charges. For more information about the books below or to view the entire NRAES catalog, visit us on the web at <WWW.NRAES.ORG>. See page 66 for NRAES contact information and office hours.

Energy Conservation for Commercial Greenhouses (NRAES-3)

Written by John W. Bartok Jr., an authority on greenhouses for over 30 years, this highly practical book, revised in 2001, reviews the merits and limitations of current energy-conservation strategies for commercial greenhouses. Topics covered in the book's 84 pages include principles of heat loss, site selection and modification, construction materials, insulation, fuels and heating, ventilation and cooling, space utilization, utilities, strategies for reducing trucking costs, and managing for efficiency. Supplementing the text are 53 illustrations, 26 tables, equations, and calculation examples. (2001)

Facilities for Roadside Markets (NRAES-52)

Selling horticultural products from a roadside market can be satisfying and profitable, but only with careful planning. This 32-page guide is valuable for persons considering a roadside market or looking to improve or expand an existing market. Three chapters cover site considerations (visibility and accessibility, utilities, drainage, zoning, and building ordinances); market layout (areas for sales, preparation, and shipping and receiving); and market structure and facilities (parking, lighting, fire protection, security, and more). Also included are 26 illustrations, four tables, and two sets of plans. (1992)

Greenhouse Engineering (NRAES-33)

This manual includes information needed to plan, construct, and control the commercial greenhouse. Major sections describe various structures, methods of materials handling, the greenhouse environment, and energy conservation. Other topics include plans for noncommercial greenhouses, access for the handicapped, and remodeling existing greenhouses. A large appendix includes conversion tables, worksheets for performing calculations, and sources of greenhouse construction materials and contractors. The manual is 212 pages long and includes over 100 line drawings. (1994)

Greenhouses for Homeowners and Gardeners (NRAES-137)

This 214-page book contains eight chapters that discuss greenhouse basics, selecting a greenhouse, planning, framing materials and glazing, layouts and equipment, the greenhouse environment, window greenhouses and growth chambers, and garden structures. It will help aspiring and practicing greenhouse operators make informed decisions about foundations, glazing and framing materials, space utilization, interior design, heating and cooling systems, supplemental lighting, watering and fertilizing systems, and other design and construction issues. The book features ten diverse do-it-yourself plans for greenhouses and other garden structures and nearly 150 line drawings. (2000)

Herbaceous Perennials Production: A Guide from Propagation to Marketing (NRAES-93)

This 220-page book is a comprehensive information source that considers the diversity of situations encountered by perennial growers in businesses of all sizes. Key chapters in the book discuss production systems and schedules, propagation (including media, nutrients, environmental requirements, and methods); plug production; transplant and seedling care; nursery and field production; pest control (including deer and small animals); and forcing out-of-season bloom. Practical discussions about starting a business, marketing and customer service, setting prices for plants, and designing a production facility are included as well. Appendixes detail propagation methods and requirements for hundreds of species, optimum germination conditions for specific perennials and biennials, pests and diseases, and useful calculations and conversions. Thirty-eight figures, 45 tables, and a glossary supplement the text. (1998)

Turfgrass Problems: Picture Clues and Management Options (NRAES–125)

This 214-page pocket guide includes over 130 color photos to help in identifying problems that affect cool-season turfgrasses. The compact, spiral-bound guide covers problems caused by nonliving (abiotic) or living (biotic) factors. The abiotic section describes 18 chemical, physical, and mechanical types of damage that can lead to turfgrass injury or death. The biotic portion covers diseases, insects, and weeds. Each problem discussion includes photos, a detailed description, conditions under which the problem tends to occur, and nonchemical management strategies. Other features include a chapter on scouting and sampling procedures; symptom timelines that tell when a certain disease, insect, or weed is likely to emerge; and a glossary. (2001)

Water and Nutrient Management for Greenhouses (NRAES–56)

To manage a greenhouse for zero runoff, certain skills are essential, including preparing stock solutions for proportioners; selecting substrate; interpreting leaf, substrate, and water test results; and estimating crop nutrient needs. This 110-page book will help greenhouse managers learn these skills. It begins with discussions on general crop needs, balancing nutrient applications with crop demand, and the units used in measuring fertilizer quantities. Subsequent chapters go into more detail about specific components of the root zone: water, fertilizer, substrate, temperature, and the biotic environment. Fifty-three tables and 15 figures supplement the text. (1996)

Workforce Management for Farms and Horticultural Businesses: Finding, Training, and Keeping Good Employees (NRAES–117)

This conference proceedings includes 14 papers that focus on creating a work environment that motivates employees and is productive, profitable, safe, and worker-friendly. Individual papers cover topics like the value of good employees, implementing people-oriented management, enhancing the employer's reputation, communicating the business's mission, managing a multicultural workforce, performance feedback, recruitment and hiring, leadership skills, elements of an employee contract, discrimination, essential regulations, worker protection standards, and developing a safety training program. (1999)

About NRAES

NRAES, the Natural Resource, Agriculture, and Engineering Service, is a not-for-profit, university-based program dedicated to assisting member university faculty in increasing the public availability of research- and experience-based knowledge. NRAES is sponsored by 14 land grant universities (see map below) and is 85% funded by user fees, including book sales and conference registration fees. All NRAES activities are guided by faculty from member land grant universities.

NRAES began in 1974 through an agreement among the cooperative extension programs in the Northeast. The program is guided by the NRAES Committee, which consists of a representative from each member university, the NRAES director, and an administrative liaison appointed by the Northeast Cooperative Extension Directors Committee.

Currently, NRAES has published more than 100 books on topics such as general agriculture, agrichemical handling, horticulture, integrated crop management, greenhouse, composting, and home. Contact us for more information and a free publications catalog.

Natural Resource, Agriculture, and Engineering Service (NRAES)
Cooperative Extension
PO Box 4557
Ithaca, New York 14852-4557
Phone: (607) 255-7654
Fax: (607) 254-8770
E-mail: nraes@cornell.edu
Web site: www.nraes.org

Marty Sailus, NRAES Director
Jeffrey S. Popow, NRAES Managing Editor

NRAES Member Universities

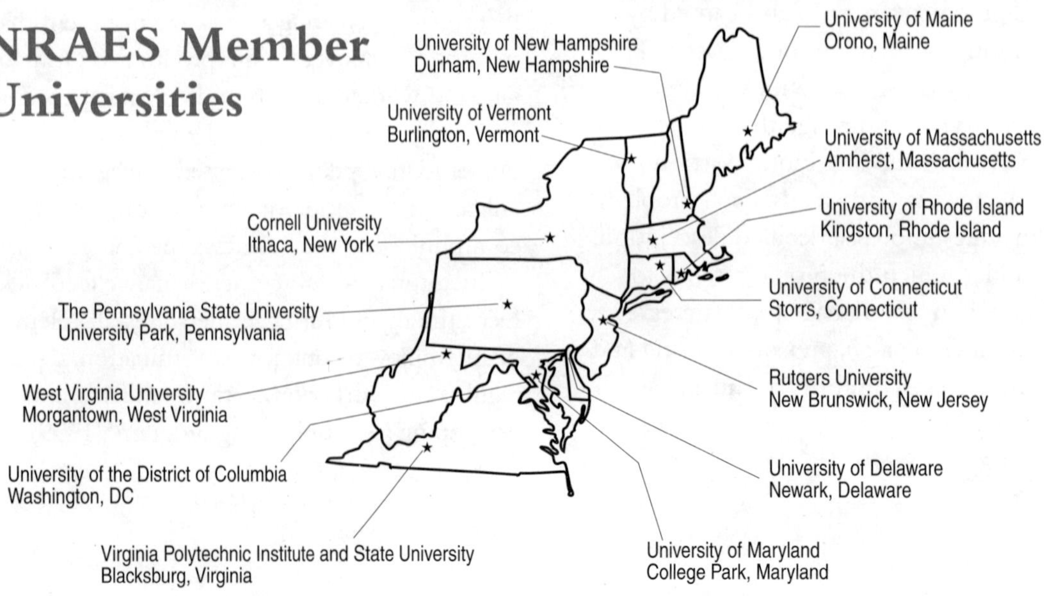